EDITOR: MARTIN WINDROW

OSPREY MILITARY

ELITÉ SERIES

35

EARLY SAMURAI
200-1500 AD

Text by
ANTHONY J BRYANT
Colour plates by
ANGUS McBRIDE

Published in 1991 by
Osprey Publishing Ltd
59 Grosvenor Street, London W1X 9DA
© Copyright 1991 Osprey Publishing Ltd

British Library Cataloguing in Publication Data
Bryant, Anthony J.
    Early Samurai: 200–1500 - (Elite Series v. 35)
    1. Japan. Armies. History
    I. Title   II. McBride, Angus   III. Series
355.00952

    ISBN 1-85532-131-9

Filmset in Great Britain
Printed through Bookbuilders Ltd, Hong Kong

Author's note

Although this book is primarily about the military
class in Japan and their equipment, the term 'samurai'
will not appear until near the end. The term appeared
rather late; a more ancient word was *mononofu*. More
commonly used throughout the mediaeval period was
the word *bushi*, *mononofu* falling out of general use
around the 1100s. Even in the 17th century we find an
occasional reference to *mononofu*, but by then it had
the same flavour as the word 'warrior' would when
used to refer to, say, a Green Beret or a member of the
SAS.

   Note that all Japanese names in this work appear in
Japanese order: surname first, given name last.

Acknowledgements

It would have been impossible to produce this book
without the help and understanding of the owner and
management of the Japan Costume Museum, Kyôto;
the friendship of the gang at Yoroi no Kozan-do,
Tokyo; and the kind assistance of and patient
conversations with fellow members of the Japanese
Society for Research and Preservation of Arms and
Armour.

Dedication

For Bruce Cohen (a.k.a. Aaron Breck Gordon), for
long friendship and shared interests; and for the
membership of the Society for Creative Anachronism.

For a catalogue of all books published by Osprey Military
please write to:

**The Marketing Manager,
Consumer Catalogue Department,
Osprey Publishing Ltd,
Michelin House, 81 Fulham Road,
London SW3 6RB**

EARLY SAMURAI 200-1500 AD

THE PROTO-HISTORIC PERIOD

Japan's palaeolithic culture lasted until around 10,000 BC, when a culture now called Jômon (after a distinctive design used on their pottery) emerged. This was a hunter-gatherer society, which was replaced in *c.* 300 BC by a society called Yayoi (after the location where their pottery was first unearthed). The Yayoi people led an elaborate agricultural life, and had well-developed regional politics.

There are no written records in Japanese of either of these societies. Most of what we know about early Japan we glean from ancient Chinese chronicles, the best of which is the *Wei Chih* of the Wei Dynasty, written in the 3rd century AD. At that time, near the end of the Yayoi Period, the *Wei Chih* makes references to trade with Wa (Japan), which they alternatively called the 'Queen Country', ruled by a warrior priest-queen named Himiko (or Pimiko), who is supposed to have united 28 neighbouring countries or tribes into a confederation under her control. Her land was called Yamataikoku, or the Country of Yamatai.

Many archaeologists and anthropologists have since wondered where this Yamataikoku could have been, and indeed the debate has become a virtual industry. There are two principal schools of thought, one placing the Wa capital in what is now northern Kyûshû, and the other placing it on Honshû, in the Kinki region (the area around modern Ôsaka, Kyôto and Nara). Let us consider the claims. The *Wei Chih* refers to Wa weaponry thus: 'When they fight, they use a halberd, shield, and a bow of wood. The bow is short in one half and long in the other. Their arrows are of bamboo, and the heads are of iron or bone.' Over 370 bronze halberd blades from the Yayoi

Period have been unearthed in Kyûshû, and only ten in Kinki. Nearly 100 iron arrowheads have been found in Kyûshû, and less than 25 in Kinki and the Kantô (Tôkyô plain). Almost 30 iron swords have been uncovered in Kyûshû, and only five in the Kansai and Kantô. It is fairly clear that the seat of Himiko's power was, in fact, in Kyûshû.

Her rule was popularly supported, and her power was great due to her mastery of '*kidô*' or the 'way of the demons'. She was doubtless a shaman of considerable power and influence. She came to the throne (or took it) in 189. Most sources say she did so while still in her early teens, for what is amazing is that even recent history books list her as having died in 260: this means, if true, that she was a phenomenal 68 years on the throne.

After becoming queen, she was attended to by 1,000 servants—only one of whom was male—to bring messages, food and drink. After establishing control she withdrew into a strongly defended palisaded fortress, and no one ever saw her again save her servants. Instead, all her appearances were handled by a younger brother who co-ruled with her, dealing with the affairs of state; she had neatly divided her rule into political and spiritual bases, setting up a pattern which would re-emerge centuries later.

The *Wei Chih* records her first encounter with the Chinese, in the summer of 239, when she sent emissaries to the Wei emperor Ming, who granted her the title *Ch'in-wei Wo Wang*—'Wa ruler friendly to Wei'. He also sent her many gifts. Six years later the Chinese bestowed a military title on her envoy, suggesting that fighting had already begun between Himiko's Yamatai and a neighbouring land called Kona (or Kunu)—possibly a rebellion.

The war was apparently going against Himiko, as the *Wei Chih* says abruptly that she died, and makes no mention of the outcome of the struggle. A huge tumulus was built for her (it has not been identified with any certainty, but there is a good claim for a large one in Kyûshû), and over 100 servants followed her in death. The historian Saeki Arikiyo has speculated that she was ritually killed by subordinate chieftains when the tide of battle turning against them was viewed as a sign of her waning magical powers. There was a brief attempt by a male to take power, but he was almost immediately replaced by a woman named Queen Iyo.

When the Yoshinogari ruins, the remains of a large Yayoi settlement, were unearthed in February 1989, there was speculation that Himiko's capital had at last been found. Others feel that it was only the seat of one of her vassal states, as its size could not have been large enough for Himiko's stature; it does, however, feature some of the structures mentioned in the Wei Chronicle.

Judging by archaeological evidence, the centre of power shifted at some point to the Kinki region. It is likely that those who ruled in Honshû in the 4th century—the Yamato—were actual lineal descendants of those who had held sway in Kyûshû during the years of the Wei intercourse a few centuries before.

One of the more tantalising ancient puzzles is that of the *dôtoku*, bells of curious shape believed to have been used in religious rituals which, though dating to the late Yayoi Period, have never been found in Kyûshû, while 200 have been unearthed in the Kansai. The *Wei Chih* makes no reference to them, despite their obvious importance to that society— another indication that Yamataikoku was not in that area. The way in which they were all buried conveniently near the surface and in relatively easily found places, some even still in their moulds, suggests that they were hidden quickly, perhaps in response to an invasion.

It is more than likely that the cause was the migration of the militant Yamato people, who, as archaeological finds indicate, possessed superior weapons and technology. As early as the *Wei Chih* people from Wa are recorded as having travelled to Korea for iron, and it is stated that by the later Yayoi Period iron sickles had become plentiful enough to replace stone reaping knives. Since we know that warfare played an important part in Yayoi Japan—at least in Yamataikoku—it is only logical to assume that some of that iron was quickly turned into swords and armour, though their principal metal was bronze until the 5th or 6th century.

The Yamato Sun Line

The 'official' establishment of the Japanese Imperial Court is attributed in the *Kojiki* and *Nihon Shoki* (the first two domestic histories written in Japanese) to the Emperor Kamu Yamato Iware Biko (a.k.a. Jinmu Tennô) who left Kyûshû for Honshû in 667 BC. After a few years of travel, subduing local warrior clans on the way, his first court was established at a place called Kashiwabara just south of present-day Nara. Although historically unreliable, the account of the relocation of the 'court' is doubtless based upon truth, but refers to a migration of *circa* AD 350, not 667 BC (although there *are* some ancient Imperial tumuli in Kashiwabara—some of the oldest).

The *Kojiki* and *Nihon Shoki* were compiled in 711 and 720 respectively. Considering that they were the first histories of Japan written by natives, they should have been valuable sources; but, alas, they are highly unreliable on matters before the 6th century. Their antinomy is a difficult problem for the historian as well, as they give different dates and ages for everything and everyone. They are even internally inconsistent, a classic case being the *Nihon Shoki* mentioning that the brother of Yamato Takeru was born in the twelfth year of the Emperor Keikô, yet in the fourth year—eight years before his birth—he was supposed to have seduced the daughter of Minotsukuri-kao. Both are full of such contradictions.

Notwithstanding references in domestic chronicles to Emperors ruling Japan in the centuries before the birth of Christ, by the mid-4th century AD there was certainly a royal family of some sort holding at least a limited autocratic power in an apparently more-or-less unified nation. This ruling line has been called the Yamato Sun Line, probably originally a *primus inter pares* which grew out of the *uji* (roughly translatable as 'clan', but more literally a community of relatives and subordinates represented and headed by a single leader) extant from the latter Yayoi days (after AD 100). It is likely to have been 28 *uji* that Himiko ruled, and it is further possible that the Yamato Sun Line was one of the lines that defeated or overthrew her. When one takes into account that one of the few historically verifiable people in ancient Japanese history—Himiko—is not mentioned in either of the two domestic historical chronicles written only about 500 years after her death, and which seek to glorify the ruling line, one may wonder about her omission (unless, of course, she had been relegated to the status of deity).

The name Yamato Sun Line was applied to the ruling house based upon their claim of descent from Amaterasu Ômikami, the sun goddess; interestingly enough, Himiko means, in archaic Japanese, 'child of the sun'. The line eventually won full control, and began assigning specific duties to each of the other *uji*, e.g. to provide goods or services to their ruling house. The Soga, a family which would later grow to amazing power, were in charge of taxes. The Naka-tomi were priests, the Inbe were diviners, the Mononobe were the professional soldiers, the Ôtomo were hereditary palace guards, and so on. Early succession to the Imperial throne was set by a consensus of *uji* heads, and as the *uji* had the honour

Evidence indicates that very few tankô *were made with scale skirts and shoulder protection, but this is still a very good reconstruction of a late-period model. The gilding is unusual. Note the high-rising rear of the* tankô. *(Japan Costume Museum)*

of contributing wives to the Imperial line they all had a stake in selecting offspring related to their own lines. This system ended up producing some minor but bloody succession conflicts.

Rise of the Yamato State

The account of the migration from Kyûshû has the Yamato people fighting with local chieftains of tribes that they called barbarians (in the classic sense—i.e., a people whose language they didn't understand). They also called the enemy 'earth-spiders', and '*Emishi*'. As Emishi is a name by which the Ainu

then suggested a fencing bout; imagine the surprise of the other upon finding that his sword, which he had just received from Yamato Takeru, was wooden. He was even more surprised when his head landed on the ground a few feet away a moment later. After many other great adventures Yamato Takeru finally died a lingering death after his heel touched a venomous dragon. Yamato Takeru, the solitary wandering hero who conquered all enemies except the supernatural, is the ultimate hero from the ancient period.

As evidenced by his tale, the Yamato and a people called Kumaso were incessantly at war. It has been suggested that the Kumaso were a South Sea people, or perhaps of the same stock as the Yamato, but not blessed with the proximity to Korea that the Yamato

This keikô is typical of the 7th and 8th centuries. (Japan Costume Museum)

would later be known, and the word itself is an archaic cognate form of the Ainu word for 'man', these must have been the ancestors of the Ainu, the caucasoid aboriginals of northern Japan.

The legendary Yamato Takeru is the archetype for Yamato heroes. There is no empirical evidence that he ever existed, but the adventures of this son of Emperor Keikô are recounted in the *Kojiki*. At the age of 16 he was sent to subdue the rebellious Kumaso in Kyûshû. Disguising himself as a lady, he allowed himself to be introduced to the rebel chieftains. During a banquet at which the chieftains drank themselves into a stupor, Yamato Takeru pulled out a concealed blade and, like the Biblical Rebecca, ended the rebellion then and there.

On the way home he tricked another enemy leader into switching swords (as a sign of friendship) and

The Yayoi city at Yoshinogari has been reconstructed. Is it the remains of Himiko's capital, or that of one of her vassals?

had enjoyed. There is no record of incompatibility of language with the Kumaso, unlike the Emishi, so the latter is the more likely.

The government of this proto-Japan, the Yamato court, was so well structured by the later mid-4th century that it had both extended its hegemony into Honshû, establishing its seat there, and was in Korea trying to fill the political vacuum brought about by the fall of China's Wei dynasty a century earlier. In 366 Japan launched a full-scale invasion of the Korean Peninsula, possibly led by the militant regent-Empress Jingû Kôgô, who is supposed to have led a Korean invasion in AD 200, according to domestic histories. No such invasion appears in Korean or Chinese chronicles, though one mentioned in 366 fits the account laid out in the *Nihon Shoki*. They forced the king of Paekche to submit, and extracted an oath from him that he would send tributes each year to the Yamato court. They also managed to occupy and establish a base of operations—though whether actually a functioning colony or only a military base is uncertain—in Mimana (Kaya in Japanese), near what is now Pusan. By 391 they were successfully engaged against Koguryŏ and Silla—the other two Korean kingdoms—on behalf of the king of Paekche, penetrating as far as modern Pyong-yang. In 404 Japan again launched an attack, this time on Koguryŏ.

The Kôfun Period and the Five Kings of Wa

In the late 4th or early 5th century the Yamato began building monumental tombs for their departed élite. One of the best indications of the socio-political hegemony of the Yamato is the fairly even distribution of these tumuli (called *kôfun* in Japanese, lending the name *Kôfun Jidai*—'Age of Burial Mounds'—to the era) throughout Honshû and Kyûshû. Earlier *kôfun* often contained jade ornaments, bronze weapons and mirrors, the latter

Not all shôkakufû kabuto were made with triangular plates, as this one excavated from the Marozuka Kôfun indicates. Note the unusual scalloped visor. (Courtesy Agency for Cultural Affairs)

Chinese imports, while later *kôfun*, particularly those of the 5th century (the peak of that era) show an advance in that most weapons and armour emerge as iron, with bronze tending to be limited to religious or ritual objects.

Buried around tombs, ringing them, were figurines called *haniwa*. There are many different designs, ranging from simple tube- or pipe-shaped sections to houses, horses, and armoured warriors. It has been theorised that the *raison d'être* for *haniwa* was to prevent soil erosion around the raised-earth tumuli; and that the oldest *haniwa* were the simplest ones, the makers eventually fashioning them more ornately.

During the early 5th century relations with China warmed again, as is recorded in the chronicles of the Han dynasty, the *Hou Han Shu*. Several emperors of the Yamato court sent representatives to the Han court, and were granted the title 'Antô Shôgun Wakoku-Ô'—'Great General of the East, King of Wa'. This obviously put the Yamato Emperor in a subject position to the Chinese Emperor, but there is no indication of this implied status causing any problems. Interestingly enough, neither of the domestic histories makes mention of this. This also serves to underscore the fact that these early emperors were more than the inactive recluses they would later become: they were warriors, too.

There were five 'Kings of Wa' who were so entitled, named in the *Hou Han Shu* as San, Chin, Sei, Kô, and Bu. These were obviously Chinese pronunciations of their Japanese names, so they do not appear in the Japanese texts, but analysis of the alternate readings of the characters of the names of the seven Japanese Emperors during that era show that they were likely to have been Emperors Ôjin, Nintoku, Hanzei, Ankô, and Yûryaku. The first envoy was sent by Emperor Ôjin, the son of Jingû Kôgô of Korean invasion fame, in 421.

Tombs of this period begin to show the first signs of horse-trappings, so it is likely that they were introduced to Japan from the continent sometime shortly after the invasions of the later 4th century. This changed the face of Japanese warfare: heretofore they had fought on foot with great infantry movements, phalanxes, and shield walls—now there was a new element.

Shields had been excavated from some earlier tumuli, but they were no more to be found. Considering the size of these shields (at 4 ft. or more in height, they were more like pavises than shields) it is no wonder that the now mounted warriors eschewed them in favour of mobility. The main weapons, until now halberds, pole-adzes, lances, and swords, became the bow and sword. Even the style of armour began to undergo a change inspired by the scale armours worn on the continent; such harnesses were more flexible, and far more comfortable when on horseback. During this century what military activity there was consisted primarily of excursions to the north to beat back the Emishi; there was little in the way of civil strife, so the changes came slowly at first.

As the years passed, the base in Mimana became more and more Korean. In 512 four prefectures of Mimana were handed over by forces less loyal to Yamato than to Korea. At about this time Paekche began feeling renewed pressure from Silla and Koguryŏ and pleaded with the Yamato court to send help. In 513 Paekche sent Confucian scholars to Japan; with them came books, and writing was introduced to the islands.

Mimana was soon under siege by Silla: the strong pro-Korean fifth column was operating openly, and the base was in danger of falling. Before help for Mimana and Paekche could come from the Yamato court, Iwai, governor of Tsukushi (a semi-autonomous Kumaso region in Kyûshû), entered into an alliance with pro-Korean forces in Silla and Mimana to stop Japanese troops from leaving Kyûshû.

Mononobe no Arakabi, head of the warrior clan, was sent to quell this test of Imperial power. Iwai's rebellion was successfully terminated (as was Iwai), but too late for Mimana, which despite an infusion of new blood under the leadership of the Ôtomo finally fell to Silla in 562. There had been enough time to save Mimana, but for some reason the Yamato court never sent the amount of aid needed. This was a period when Paekche needed Japan's help in protecting itself against Silla, and Japan simply weakened itself excessively by attempting a two-front conflict. The only thing that averted total disaster was disunity in China.

The Buddhist Revolution

During the Mimana struggles against Silla, Paekche sent many presents to Japan. In 538 a gift from King Songmyong of Paekche arrived which was to change the course of history: Buddhist statues and sutras. Just as one cannot discuss European history without mentioning the Church, one likewise cannot discuss Japan and ignore the great social upheaval brought by Buddhism.

The king of Silla recommended the religion in glowing terms, his own land having accepted it as early as 384. The Imperial clan immediately took to the new religion, while several clans opposed it, leading to violent confrontations. The Nakatomi, with vested interests as intercessors with the gods, were strongly opposed, as were the Mononobe; the latter, however, opposed the religion simply because it was foreign, not from any religious fervour. They were among the first Japanese militant nationalists. Where temples and Buddhist images were constructed, the Mononobe put them to the torch.

The line was quickly drawn between the forces of chauvinistic conservatism and those of social reform. Although power politics were a major factor, true religious feelings should not be left out of the picture, as Buddhism acquired some serious adherents. The struggle lasted on and off for almost 50 years.

The Soga, headed by Great Minister Iname, were quick to side with the new religion, gaining the benefit of Imperial favour. As the Soga were already inextricably linked with the Yamato court this move

This mabizashi-tsuke kabuto *seems to have been gilded originally. It is typical for this style of helmet, and was part of the* armour haul from the Marozuka Kôfun. The shikoro *did not survive. (Courtesy Agency for Cultural Affairs)*

only served to strengthen the ties. Soga no Umako, son and successor (assuming office in 570) of Iname, obtained the Emperor's permission to worship the Buddha and built a small chapel for his own use. When Emperor Yômei, who had declared himself for the new religion, died suddenly in 587, the clouds burst. Mononobe no Moriya gathered his allies and attempted to put a prince of their faction on the throne. Umako, leading an army of supporters, met and annihilated the Mononobe at the Battle of Mt. Shigi. With the militant Mononobe crushed the Nakatomi offered no threat, and the Soga placed their own man on the throne as Emperor Sujun.

Umako, not as pious as his cause would indicate, later had Sujun assassinated, elevating his own niece, Suiko, to the throne as a reigning Empress. As prince regent he named a son of Sujun's predecessor, Yômei. The son was later to be known as Shôtoku Taishi, the greatest proponent of Buddhism and one of the greatest reformers in Japan's history, and, though he would never live to mount the throne, one of its most influential figures.

In 604 he issued the Constitution of Seventeen Articles, a set of strict moral principles. He also set about propagating the religion widely throughout the land; and instituted several reforms including new

9

systems of court rank, eliminating some of the titles that had been in vogue during the Mononobe/Soga/Nakatomi struggles.

Shôtoku was also able to send an envoy to China in 607, who returned with a Chinese counterpart. Diplomatic and cultural missions continued for years, Japanese scholars travelling to China to study Buddhism while Chinese scholars came to Japan to teach.

THE HISTORICAL PERIOD

The Asuka Era, named for the city that served as the imperial seat, began upon Shôtoku Taishi's appointment as regent in 593. The Asuka period was marked most notably by the Sinification of Japan, as the Japanese adopted first the Chinese writing system, then the Chinese Imperial court structure, Chinese clothing, Chinese art, and almost the very Chinese lifestyle itself.

Also adopted was the concept of a reclusive Emperor less involved in day-to-day administration; bureaucrats and officials would see to that. Heretofore there was no shortage of emperors and Imperial princelings to don armour and take the field, but hereafter they would—with a few notable exceptions—remain behind the curtains, perhaps giving military orders but seldom taking up the sword. This was the age of Shôtoku Taishi.

After the death of Empress Suiko in 628 (six years after that of Shôtoku Taishi), clan leader Soga no Emishi passed over Prince Yamashiro no Ôe, the son of Shôtoku and rightful heir to the throne, in favour of Jômei. Upon the latter's death he chose Kôgyoku, the daughter of a past Emperor and a Soga clanswoman. The Grand Minister was not satisfied with deciding Imperial succession; he built for himself a tomb of Imperial proportions, and began assuming many regal prerogatives, including the allocation of high court titles (all to children and cousins). His successor, Soga no Iruka, was even worse; feeling secure enough to take on Yamashiro no Ôe, he had

This reproduction of a mabizashi-tsuke kabuto shows it in all its glory. The gilding and piercework detail around the central horizontal band and the visor, as well as the 'cup' crest and shikoro, mark it as the helmet of someone very important. (Courtesy Japan Costume Museum)

him and his entire family put to the sword. There was no one left to oppose him, yet all hated Soga no Iruka.

The Nakatomi, who through the Buddhist upheaval and the work of the Soga had lost their prestige at court, moved against Iruka in 645. Plotting with Prince Katsuragi (later Emperor Tenji) and a branch of the Soga clan, the Nakatomi sent assassins after Iruka. Although they very nearly bungled the task through fear, they managed to dispatch Iruka in the palace before the very eyes of Empress Kôgyoku. The Empress abdicated in favour of her brother Kôtoku, and Katsuragi no Ôji was named heir apparent ... but it was not to be just yet. For his part in helping Prince Katsuragi to power Nakatomi Kamatari was given the name Fujiwara and became the first of that line. In future generations the Fujiwara would come to dominate the Imperial court more completely and with more impunity than the Soga had ever achieved.

Kôtoku, prompted by Prince Katsuragi (the *de facto* ruler throughout the reigns of Kôtoku and his successor) and his chief advisor Nakatomi no Kamatari, proclaimed what has come to be called the Taika Reform, introducing the system of era names (starting with 'Taika', Great Change, hence the name). He reorganized the very structure of the government by eliminating titles and creating offices and a rigid rank structure for court officials. It was an ambitious, and successful, reformation. It was also remarkably peaceful; but then, he did have the support of most of the clan heads. The Japanese system was becoming more Chinese. One of the reforms which would have a strong influence in future generations was military conscription.

The struggles and social upheaval during the 6th and early 7th centuries had weakened the Yamato position, especially *vis-à-vis* the continent. (In 602,

for example, a planned attack on Silla was cancelled entirely due to the illness and death of leader Prince Kume.) China, now unified under the T'ang, had been beaten back by Koguryŏ in 646, but in 660 took Paekche, and a few years later made it a satrapy under a Chinese viceroy.

Empress Saimei (by a quirk of fate, 37th ruler of Japan and also the 35th on the official charts—she had ruled before under the name Kôgyoku, reclaiming the throne upon Kôtoku's death) personally led a naval expedition of some 27,000 men to liberate Paekche in 661. She died in Kyûshû en route, but this time the attack went ahead as scheduled. The Japanese were met and very nearly wiped out by a superior T'ang naval force at Paekchongang. When the remains of the fleet returned, they brought back with them from Paekche refugees including men of arts and letters, whose influence was to affect greatly the future of Japanese art. This expedition was also to mark Japan's last attempt to land armed forces in

This well-preserved tankô *was part of the Marozuka Kôfun find. It seems unusual in that rather than leather edging or binding it has turned-over edges on its plates. Note the narrow overlap of the front plate, and the two hinges on the right side. (Courtesy Agency for Cultural Affairs)*

Korea for many centuries, and the beginning of the 'defend our island' mentality: Dazaifu, the northern Kyûshû military base, suddenly became very important. Prince Katsuragi became Emperor Tenji, and the reforms went on.

A succession dispute and brief civil war made Tenji's younger brother Tenmu the Emperor, replacing Tenji's son. Tenmu proved himself an able ruler and talented administrator during his 14 years on the throne. His greatest achievement, the Taihô Code of 701, limited the bearing or ownership of arms to the military, and had all others placed under the jurisdiction of the Hyôbushô (Ministry of Military Affairs) or securely guarded by the Imperial Armoury. He remembered well how he came to the throne, and he had no desire to lose it the same way. As time passed the Code would be weakened and eventually completely ignored, but for the time being it was a genuine attempt to limit the military.

The Capital in Nara

Japanese tradition in ancient times was to move the capital when an Emperor died, due to the 'uncleanliness' of death. More frequently, at least during the Asuka period, this took the form of merely abandoning the palace and building a new one. In 710 Emperor Genmei elected to move the capital a short way from Asuka to Nara, and to establish a permanent capital. The exact reason for the choice of Nara—short of its proximity to several major temples—is unclear, as the city is not as well situated in relation to the sea as earlier capitals had been.

The Buddhist clergy became more and more powerful in Nara, even to the extent that one proto-Rasputin priest named Dôkyô acquired such influence with an ex-Empress who had ascended the throne as reigning Empress Shôtoku that he nearly got himself named as the Imperial successor. The

This reconstruction of a poncho-style ushikake-shiki, *made sometime before 1942 by Suenaga Masao, is a superb example of the armours of the 8th and 9th centuries. Like all photographs of his work it is necessarily copied from a poor quality original. (Suenaga,* Nihon Jôdai no Katchû)

Fujiwara, who had replaced the Soga as Imperial controllers, had him banished after her death, and convened a council to consider the issue of women on the throne. They decided that never again would an Empress rule in her own right (and save for two powerless women during the Edo Era, none have).

Fujiwara Nakamaro, the powerful and ambitious head of the clan, built up the military by improving frontier defences. It was also he who began the process of separating a military and a peasant class by preferring the use of professional warriors over the conscription called for in the Taika Reforms, and brought about a further dilution of the Taihô Code. Japan now had professional military men, as well as militarily-minded clans.

THE CAPITAL AT HEIANKYÔ

Partly out of frustration born of clerical meddling in civil affairs, Emperor Kanmu ordered the capital moved in 794; and a new capital was established called Heiankyô (Capital of Peace and Tranquillity), later to be called Kyôto. The city was laid out in a grid, modelled after the T'ang capital of Ch'ang-an. Kyôto would be the capital—if not functionally, at least legally—until the Emperor moved to Tôkyô in 1879. Although the actual governing structure would at times be in Kamakura or other towns, the Emperor and the seat of the nation were in Kyôto.

Surrounding the city are mountains, and upon them were built many great Buddhist temples and monasteries, some of which would vex the city and the court more than they ever had at Nara.

The Militant Buddhist Clergy

As the Buddhist clergy's influence continued to grow, they managed to become a military power. The concept of a Buddhist 'church militant' began in 970 when monasteries began employing groups of armed men to defend their holdings. These bands were virtual private armies, and only a small minority were actually members of the clergy. Intra-sect strife—as well as inter-family strife (clans tended to support and be connected with a single temple or group of

temples)—was a serious problem, and the different sects were ever ready to argue their positions with the assistance of a sword point. Many temples were not above putting rival temples to the torch. Larger, wealthier temples naturally had better armies.

As the power of the temples grew they began to attempt to influence court policy. The Tendai-sect temple on Mt. Hiei had an army of *sôhei* (warrior monks) numbering several thousand, and between 981 and the start of the Genpei War in 1180 made many forays down the mountain into Kyôto to press their demands. While some were little more than brigands, most *sôhei* were well organised. They also had their share of valiant warriors and gifted commanders, though on the whole their main advantage was in numbers.

The Rise of the Provincial Clans

While the temples were becoming stronger, so were the military houses outside Kyôto. During the 8th and 9th centuries officials living in the provinces began consolidating their power. Though living away from the central government meant that they had no choice but to forgo the luxuries and lifestyles enjoyed by their counterparts in the capital, they found that their autonomy—often, ironically, supported by the central government's myopic *laissez-faire* attitude— was an admirable compensation. They were laying the groundwork for future provincial warrior families with great powers.

As the Fujiwara had a virtual stranglehold on the capital, controlling every office and position including *kanpaku*, the highest civil position, most of these provincial lords were not Fujiwara; and naturally not a few of them had no liking for the power-monopolising grandees. One of the differences was that the Fujiwara were aristocrats, not warriors. Though many were able to distinguish themselves in martial endeavours, they are now best known as men of letters.

When the ambitions of these clans were added to their power (for it must be remembered that not a few heads of great provincial families were descendants of the Imperial family) a dangerous situation was brewing. The court's virtual ignorance of the provinces only fuelled the anger. One of the first tests of the power of these provincial lords was the rise and rebellion of Taira no Masakado.

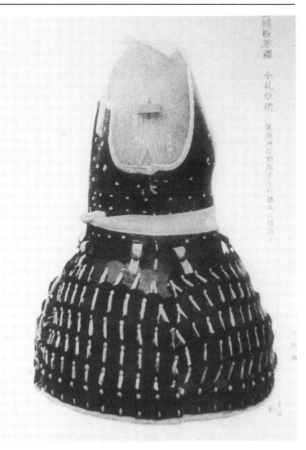

Suenaga's reconstruction of the scale-skirted tankô *shows well its hourglass shape, and the attachment of the shoulder straps. (Suenaga, Nihon Jôdai no Katchû)*

Masakado, great-great grandson of Emperor Kanmu, was based in the Kantô area and served the Fujiwara. He wanted the office of *kebiishi* (essentially head of the national police, an office whose commands carried Imperial authority); and upon refusal of that title retired to his home states and began a guerrilla war against 'the establishment'. In 935 he slew his uncle, the governor of Hitachi. His other uncles and cousins struck back, but were defeated and had to retreat to Kyôto.

Masakado is revered in the Tokyo area as a kind of Robin Hood, a man fighting for the rights of the provincials against the Imperial institutions which used them only as a rice basket. He claimed the title of *Heishin-ô* (New Emperor Taira) in 939, going so far as to make government appointments. Finally the Imperial court had had enough. He had promised the office of *kanpaku* to Fujiwara Sumitomo, who raised his own flag of rebellion, forcing the Imperially-sent troops to fight a two-front conflict.

Masakado and Sumitomo were both eventually killed and their heads sent back to Kyôto for viewing. According to legend, Masakado's head is supposed to have leapt up from the viewing platform and flown back to the grounds of Kanda Jinja, where it was buried with honour. His grave remains in the same spot in what is now Tokyo, a stone's throw from the Imperial Palace. The irony would not escape Masakado, who never got so close in his life.

The court in Kyôto finally noticed the provincial clans, and resolved never again to underestimate their power and determination; rather, it decided to utilise their skills and energies. When territorial governor Abe no Yoritoki rebelled in 1055, Minamoto Yoriyoshi was promptly called from his home in the north-east provinces to solve the problem. The conflict, called the 'Early Nine Years' War', ended in 1063. Yoriyoshi's son, Yoriie, was called out to subdue Yoritoki's successor several years later in the 'Later Three Years' War'. The Imperial court refused to grant funds to him afterwards, however, forcing him to pay rewards and make gratuities to those who helped him from Minamoto coffers. This helped strengthen ties between the Minamoto and allied clans, and gained them popular support. It also showed everyone how far out of touch the court was with society outside the gates of Kyôto.

The Rise of Heike

The first clash of the Genji (literally 'Minamoto clan') and the Heike (literally 'Taira family') occurred in 1108, when Taira Masamori was sent out to punish Minamoto Yoshichika in Kyûshû. The Taira had made a name for themselves in the south subduing pirates and brigands, while the Minamoto made theirs in the north fighting rebels. It was natural that they would eventually clash. A subsequent confrontation came in 1128, when a Taira clan member killed the governor of Awa and Minamoto Yorinobu was sent to subduc him. Yorinobu entrenched in what had been Taira territory, paving the way for vengeance that would take a century to come.

The 1156 Hôgen no Ran, or Hôgen Era Insurrection, was brought about through a power struggle between Emperor Go-Shirakawa and retired Em-

Suenaga's reconstruction of a shôkakufû kabuto. *Note the construction of the beaked section; it was quite solid. (Suenaga,* Nihon Jôdai no Katchû)

peror Sutoku, who wished to re-mount the throne. Sutoku's army was wiped out in the few but bloody conflicts, and among his supporters were the Genji. The lone voice against Sutoku in the clan was Minamoto Yoshitomo. The Minamoto were not the only clan divided by the conflict: the Taira and even the Fujiwara clans were also split. Yoshitomo, allied as he was with Taira no Kiyomori, was ordered to lay siege to the fortress of his own father and brother, which he did. When he captured his father he begged Kiyomori for his life, but Kiyomori had his father put to death.

The Hôgen no Ran was over, but Yoshitomo was unhappy; his reward had been too small (especially when he compared it to that of Kiyomori), and Kiyomori had been the instrument of his father's death. Three years later, in 1159, he and Fujiwara Nobuyori rose in rebellion against Kiyomori in what came to be called the Heiji no Ran. They were crushed, and Yoshitomo was killed. His young sons, however, were allowed to live; and this was where Kiyomori made his great error.

One thing which disturbs readers of Japanese history is the frequent putting to death of an entire family—children included—for the transgressions of the father alone. Kiyomori's experience gave Japan the 'worst case scenario', the reason to leave not one baby alive. The three brothers he spared were Yoritomo, Noriyori, and Yoshitsune, who would overthrow the Taira and send Kiyomori's family into oblivion.

Kiyomori, supposedly a son of Emperor Shira-

There were many styles of swords used over the years. These comparative *sketches show only a few of the oldest.*

kawa, had come to power in the 1140s when he was made governor of Aki. His star rose higher when he was on the winning side in the Hôgen no Ran, and was given great titles and authority. By the end of the Heiji no Ran he enjoyed absolute power. Playing kingmaker behind the scenes, he was eventually able to put his nephew Takakura on the throne, and married Takakura to his daughter. He was named first *Naidaijin* (Home Minister) and then *Dajô Daijin* (Prime Minister and President of the Ruling Council)—the first member of a military clan to hold those offices.

Some 60 members of his family held major government posts; it was the Soga and Fujiwara all over again. He even instituted a civil intelligence corps, a group of 300 pages who were his eyes and

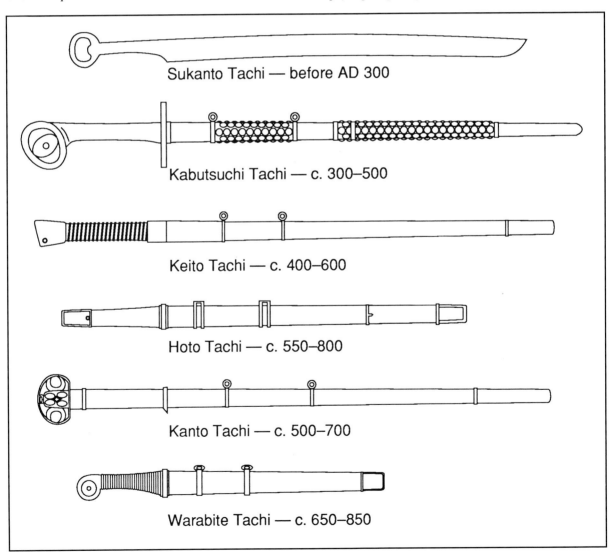

Sukanto Tachi — before AD 300

Kabutsuchi Tachi — c. 300–500

Keito Tachi — c. 400–600

Hoto Tachi — c. 550–800

Kanto Tachi — c. 500–700

Warabite Tachi — c. 650–850

ears on everything that happened, and who were consequently hated and feared. Nevertheless, he was controlled in some of his excesses by his eldest son Shigemori. It was the latter's untimely death at the age of 43 in 1179 that loosened the reins. Kiyomori imprisoned Go-Shirakawa, deposed the *kanpaku*, and forced Takakura to resign in favour of the Emperor's two-year-old son Antoku (who was Kiyomori's grandson).

The non-Taira nobles were in uproar, but under the tight Taira control there was little that they could do. Prince Mochihito, who was by-passed for the throne in favour of Kiyomori's grandson Antoku, put out a call to arms. The Genji responded.

THE GENPEI WAR

The Genpei War (named for the Chinese pronunciation of the characters making up the names Minamoto and Taira) was a struggle which deeply affected the Japanese psyche. The banners of the Minamoto were white, and the Taira red, so their red and white mean much the same to Japanese as do 'blue and grey' to Americans and 'orange and green' to the Irish.

Mochihito was quickly cornered in Nara and killed, but Yoritomo did not give up. In 1180 he sent out a call rallying the far-flung remnants of the Genji, attracting in the process many allies from clans disaffected by the excesses of Heike rule. One of those who rallied to Yoritomo's call was his younger brother, Yoshitsune. Having been brought up separately, the two had not seen each other for years. Accompanying Yoshitsune were his retainers, who included the legendary giant warrior-monk Musashi-bô Benkei. The Genji, rough, countrified warriors,

presented an obvious contrast to their softer, intellectual Heike cousins; and each looked down upon the other for those reasons.

One of the first battles of the war was between the *sôhei* of Tôdai-ji (a pro-Minamoto temple) and a detachment of Heike warriors at the Uji Bridge. Kiyomori's samurai won their engagement, but in a fit of pique had Tôdai-ji burned to the ground; over 3,500 died in the conflagration. Kiyomori died shortly after, but his sons and grandsons carried on his policies.

Yoritomo set up base in Kamakura, and sent his kin and allies out to fight on his behalf. He seldom fought himself; he was the brain behind the strategies, but most of the actual tactics he left to his able generals. In fact, without some of his commanders he would probably have lost the war.

One of Yoritomo's more enthusiastic generals was

This section of the procession of the Kyôto Jidai Matsuri (Festival of the Ages) shows warriors in what was intended to be typical Kôfun Period gear.

Except for the trousers, it is fairly accurate. The man on horseback actually dates to the Nara Period, some 400 years later than his escorts.

his cousin, Minamoto no Yoshinaka (better known as Kiso no Yoshinaka after his estate in Kiso), husband to the famous Tomoe Gozen. Both were valiant warriors, famed and feared in their own right; Tomoe Gozen had no qualms about accompanying Yoshinaka on campaign, herself armed and prepared to do battle. The rustic background of Yoshinaka and Tomoe Gozen probably played a major part in this; no Heike general's wife rode into battle, sword swinging.

For years minor skirmishes continued, and finally, in 1182, Yoshinaka entered the capital, forcing the Heike to flee with the young Emperor Antoku. His excesses in the city (perhaps exaggerated in historical texts owing to his unfamiliarity with Kyôto's rigid hierarchy and protocols) alarmed both Kyôto citizens and Yoritomo. When Yoshinaka proclaimed himself shôgun, he sealed his own fate; Yoritomo wanted the

The ô-yoroi as it appeared during the middle of the Heian Period, with all the gear that accompanied it. Note the use of only the single *kote. The protective capability of the huge* sode *is clear. (Japan Costume Museum)*

title, and as head of the Genji he regarded it as his by right.

Yoshitsune's first major campaign for his brother was the elimination of their own cousin. Yoshitsune drove Yoshinaka from the capital, and Yoshinaka was slain a few days later. Of the fate of Tomoe Gozen, no record speaks with authority: some say she killed many of Yoshinaka's attackers before fleeing to a temple and taking holy vows, praying for her husband's soul. Others say she took his head so that no one else could, and walked out into the sea to her death.

This late Heian kabuto, an Important Cultural Property, is a simple multiplate with large rivets, a style called ô-boshi. The decorative arrow-shaped strip of metal is called a shinodare, and as many as three could be seen on the front plate like this. (Private collection)

Ichi-no-Tani

Yoshitsune turned and followed the trail of the Heike. He found them encamped at a valley called Ichi-no-Tani, a naturally fortified area, with the Heike fleet at anchor in the harbour to the south, and cliffs on the north. Narrow entrances in the east and west were well guarded, so Yoshitsune decided that the best course for attack was to ride down the steep cliff face. On 18 March 1184 Yoshitsune led a small number of shock-troop cavalry in the charge. The Heike were so stunned by the attack that they moved their troops to repel it, and the rest of the Genji army poured into the valley through the unguarded passes.

The Taira made a frantic rush for their boats. During the escape a Genji samurai named Kumagai Naozane caught a well-dressed and obviously very aristocratic Heike samurai. Kumagai was about to allow the Heike noble to escape, as he was only 17 (the same age as his own son), but other Genji warriors were on his heels so Kumagai had no choice but to take his head. The young man was Taira no Atsumori, nephew of Kiyomori, and his tragic death has been a popular subject for Noh, Kabuki, and artists for generations.

After fleeing to their ships the Heike were out of range of Genji attacks. A good-natured challenge was sent to the Genji in the form of a fan at the end of a long pole. A small craft rowed to within a few hundred feet of the shore, and an archer was urged to try to shoot the fan. The Genji, knowing that success would bring great face, chose their best archer. He rode his horse into the sea up to the bridle, took careful aim, and hit the fan square on the clasp, sending it fluttering, shattered, into the waves. Both sides cheered the feat, roundly saluting the young marksman. Such was the manner of warfare in old Japan: a serious business, but one in which respect for and bantering with foes could still be found.

The Genji caught up with the Heike at Dan-no-Ura, the straits between Kyûshû and Honshû. The small fleet of the Genji almost doubled in size as clans formerly allied to the Heike switched sides. Faced with defeat, many of the Heike nobility jumped into the sea, preferring suicide to death at the hands of the Genji (or worse, being taken prisoner). Among those who perished in the waves was Emperor Antoku, accompanied by his grandmother, who told the young Emperor that they were returning to the capital, and that 'perhaps there is a capital even below the waves'.

Just before the battle Yoshitsune had had a violent argument with fellow commander Kajiwara no Kagetoki, a true villain, and the two almost drew their blades. Kagetoki wanted to command the attack, but Yoshitsune prevailed. This set the resentful Kagetoki against Yoshitsune, and he soon had reports going to Kamakura denouncing the young Minamoto as treacherous and power-hungry. Yoritomo believed him.

Yoshitsune re-entered Kyôto as a hero and was given the post of *kebiishi* by the Emperor—perhaps an attempt by the latter to split the Minamoto power base. Yoritomo was livid, and considered this to be the final straw. His brilliant young brother Yoshitsune, like Yoshinaka before him, would have to go, and it would take a Minamoto to do it; he called for his other brother, Noriyori.

Noriyori, the least well known of the brothers, was not the military genius that Yoshitsune was; yet he won some key battles. He was not the political strategist that Yoritomo was; yet he had forged alliances critical to the Genji cause. He tried to talk Yoritomo out of his planned vendetta against their young brother, even refusing to take command of the campaign against him, but Yoritomo viewed this as treason. He had Noriyori banished to the temple of Shuzenji in Izu, and later had him put to death.

Yoritomo ordered Yoshitsune's death, and the latter fled with a handful of faithful retainers. For four years they were able to evade or fight off Yoritomo's forces, but one by one they were slain. At the end there was only Benkei and Yoshitsune. While the tragic hero committed suicide, Benkei bought time for Yoshitsune with his own life. (There is an amusing legend which claims that Yoshitsune escaped across the sea to China, where he became known as Genghis Khan—his name in Chinese pronunciation is Gen Gikei.)

The ruthless, scheming Yoritomo was completely victorious; all of his enemies, real and imagined, were thrown down. In 1192 he received the appointment he so craved: the shôgunate. The age of the civil government was over; now there was a military regime, a *bakufu* or 'tent government', centred in Kamakura away from the intrigues and influences of the capital. Yoritomo completely revised the government, eliminating some offices and creating others. He proved himself an able administrator, easily maintaining control over the complex bureaucracy he had envisioned and created.

The Kamakura *Bakufu* and the Hôjô Regency

It is ironic, perhaps, that Yoritomo's wife Masako was of the Taira clan. (Technically, she was a daughter of the Hôjô, but the Hôjô clan itself was descended from Taira no Sadamori, one of those who had participated in the crushing of Masakado's rebellion in the 10th century.) In a way her behaviour after Yoritomo's death could be seen as a kind of vengeance for her distant cousins; for she sided with her own family against her husband's, even going so far as to have her own children made targets for the assassin's blade.

After Yoritomo's accidental death at the age of 52 in 1199 his 17-year-old son Yoriie became shôgun.

The samurai in full gear, circa late Kamakura Period. The armour is a replica of one said to have been owned by Hôjô Tokimune, shikken at the time of the Mongol invasion. (Courtesy Yoroi no Kôzan-dô)

Yoriie was not interested in listening to the Hôjô advisers his mother had picked, and went his own way, with the Hiki clan which had raised him for Yoritomo. The Hôjô, realising that their power was in jeopardy, began to consider desperate measures. When Yoriie fell desperately ill, they made their move.

They suggested that shôgunal powers be divided up between Sanetomo, Yoriie's brother, over whom they had influence, and Ichiman, Yoriie's infant son and preferred heir, whom they felt they could bring under their control. They sent an over-hasty letter to Kyôto announcing Yoriie's death in 1203, and asking for Imperial acceptance of the appointment of Sanetomo. Suddenly, Yoriie began to recover—and it was too late to call back the messenger.

The Hôjô immediately offered to appease the Hiki clan, guardians of Ichiman, by inviting the clan head, Yoshikazu, to their villa for a Buddhist ceremony. Though doubting the veracity of Hôjô claims, he went. He was murdered; and Hôjô troops surrounded the Hiki estates, and put every man, woman, and child to the sword before setting the buildings on fire. Among those who died was the infant Ichiman, of whom only the sleeve of one of his kimonos survived. Yoriie was banished to the Shuzenji, the same temple that briefly housed Noriyori, where Hôjô Tokimasa had him killed a year later. Sanetomo duly became shôgun.

Sanetomo acted as shôgun—under the subtle control of the Hôjô—for several years. His life ended abruptly in 1219 at the hands of his own nephew, 18-year-old Kugyô, who sought vengeance for what he saw as complicity in Yoriie's death. The Hôjô seized on the chance to conduct a virtual purge of the remaining branches and sons of the Minamoto clan, claiming their involvement in the murder of the shôgun. The Minamoto were utterly annihilated.

Retired Emperor Go-Toba, who had originally

The printing of the tsurubashiri could be very elaborate indeed; note even the deliberately different sizes of the 'dots'.

The sendan-no-ita and kyubi-no-ita are in place. Detail of Tokimune's ô-yoroi. (Courtesy Yoroi no Kôzan-dô)

bestowed the title of shôgun on Yoritomo, could no longer tolerate the *bakufu* and the Hôjô; he declared Yoshitoki a rebel and issued a call to arms. His brief war on the Hôjô took place during the Shokyû Era, and was called the Shokyû Insurrection. Despite fervent pleas, no help came from the mighty forces of the monasteries on Mt. Hiei; Go-Toba's forces were defeated soundly, leaving the Hôjô in control. For the following decades there was jockeying for position between the Imperial court and the Hôjô to put a shôgun of their camp in power. The next two were

The mittsu-kuwagata *(triple-bladed crest) on this* kabuto *are Kamakura style, but the rest of the* kabuto *is styled after those from the 15th or 16th century. (Courtesy Yoroi no Kôzan-dô)*

This modern reconstruction of a haramaki, *styled after that of the Kamakura Period, is fitted with* sode. *Note how the* gyôyô *have been made smaller to compensate and moved forward to take the place of the* sendan-no-ita *and* kyûbi-no-ita. *The lacing is called* iro-iro odoshi, *varied-colour; the top is pale green, then orange, white, two layers of purple, orange, purple, green, orange, and finally white. (Courtesy Yoroi no Kôzan-dô)*

Fujiwara, and the remaining six from the ranks of the Imperial princes.

As a point in their favour, the Hôjô rule was mostly fair and just. Honest administration was their intent, although they felt no compunction about using a puppet shôgun as their front. The Hôjô *shikken* was more of an *eminence gris*, although everyone knew that they actually held the power.

In 1232 the *bakufu* (in the person of Hôjô Yasutoki, third *shikken*) promulgated the Jôei Code, a compilation of laws for the governance of the warrior clans. It was such an efficient document that it found effect in the peasant classes as well, giving them rights and privileges they had never enjoyed before, including the right to sell their land and move.

The Hôjô slowly began to get soft; their lives were peaceful, and they enjoyed every luxury. Then disaster struck. In 1256 militant monks began lashing out at Kyôto, forcing the *bakufu* to send troops to the capital. In 1257 a terrible earthquake hit Kamakura. Two years later plague descended, continuing through the next year and coupled with famine. The people began to turn to religion.

Hônen, Shinran and Nichiren, great Buddhist leaders, rose up to offer new teachings and new ways to salvation, and bringing new problems for the *bakufu* to deal with. Hônen, of the Jôdo (Pure Land) sect, preached that the repetition of invocations to the Buddha ('*Namu Amida Butsu*', or 'Hail to Amidha Buddha') was the key. Jôdo attracted many warriors, and several surviving helmet crests today bear the etched or lacquered invocation. It also attracted common people in droves, as there was no emphasis on building temples or collecting money. Naturally, the established temples were up in arms—literally.

Nichiren went to the capital and preached hellfire, telling the aristocracy that destruction was near unless they changed their ways. Doomsayers were not welcomed by the administration in those days: he was charged with treason and banished to Sado Island—but by the time he got there the Mongols were almost on the beaches. A Mongol attack had been one of his predictions, so he was quickly pardoned and brought back to Kamakura.

THE MONGOL INVASIONS

In 1227 Kublai Khan—grandson of the great Genghis Khan, so according to Japanese legend the descendant of Yoshitsune—had succeeded in conquering China. By 1258 the Korean peninsula was his as well, and he cast his eyes towards Japan. In 1268 he sent envoys to the Japanese court demanding tribute; the embassy was sent back—but only because the court refused to deal with them, leaving all decisions in the hands of the shôgun or *shikken*. For five years this continued, until the Khan grew tired of the game.

In 1274 some 800 ships set sail from Korea, loaded with some 30,000 Mongols, Chinese, and Koreans. When they landed at Hakata in Kyûshû, Japan was in trouble. The Mongols had superior tactics; they knew how to fight in groups and units, while the

samurai were firmly entrenched in their traditions of seeking personal glory and being the first to accomplish some feat. The Mongols also possessed catapults, sending flaming and exploding missiles down on the defenders. To the samurai, used to individual ruthlessness in battle, the Mongol tactics of wholesale slaughter were shocking. Desperate pleas flew to Kamakura for assistance.

The Mongols had taken several small islands, and prospects looked bad for the native samurai; then one night, it began to rain, and a wild wind began to blow. A terrible storm arose, dashing the Mongol ships about as if they were corks in a bowl, scattering the fleet and sending scores of vessels to the bottom or smashing against the rocky shore, at the cost of thousands of lives. Barely half the fleet made it back to the continent.

The campaign was over and the enemy fleet limped home; but the *bakufu* knew that they had to expect another, and so ordered the construction of a stone wall at Hakata Bay. While the building was in progress the Khan sent another embassy demanding that the Emperor submit. This time, there was a response: the envoys were beheaded.

Finally the second invasion came, plunging the nation into feverish activity. Temples and monasteries all across the land echoed day and night with the sound of fervent prayer as priest and layman alike invoked their gods and begged for divine intervention.

The Mongols' second fleet was much larger than the first, and divided into two, one part setting out from South China and one from Korea. There were reputedly over 200,000 men in 4,000 ships. Were it not for the jealousy of one of the commanders (who refused to wait for the other) they might well have succeeded in their invasion, but fortunately for Japan they landed several days apart, in August 1281.

The wall at Hakata held, allowing small Japanese ships to dart out and harry the larger ships of the Mongol fleet. No matter how hard they tried, the Mongols could not make a landing in any force. The ships were soon in dire straits; it was the middle of a hot summer, they were running out of food, and much of what they had had gone bad. Disease began to spread through the fleet. Meanwhile the samurai continued to harass the Mongol ships. For all their efforts, though, the outcome was grimly predictable:

when the Mongols finally decided to accept the risks and losses and land, then they would, and nothing could stop their overwhelming numbers.

Then it happened again: the day after a retired Emperor made the pilgrimage to Ise to personally entreat the intercession of his ancestor the sun goddess at her great shrine, the winds came, worse than before. This was the *kami kaze*, the spirit wind; and even the Mongols with their superior weapons and tactics were no match for the gods of Japan. This time, a full two-thirds of the invasion force failed to return. The Khan was prevented from raising a third army and fleet.

Ironically, this victory was to prove the undoing of the *bakufu*. Traditionally, after a successful campaign the *bakufu* would have awarded land and money to those who had played a part in the victory. This time, however, there was no conquered land, and no gold came into the shogunal coffers. In fact, immense amounts had gone out already—and now the people wanted their rewards. Among those demanding a share of the nonexistent spoils were the priests. After all, who else could take the credit for a divine victory? Surely not the soldiers. There was also famine in the land, as farming had unavoidably been neglected during the invasion crisis.

The Fall of the Hôjô

The victory against the Mongols was largely due to the foresight and capable administration of the sixth *shikken*, Hôjô Tokimune, but his efforts had exhausted him, and he died in 1284 at the early age of 34. Tokimune had been one of the ablest and most conscientious of the *shikken*; and now that Japan needed a firm but just hand, she got only disaster.

This haramaki *dates from the Kamakura Period. Its design, making no allowances for* sode, *means one of two things: it was armour for a retainer, or 'undress' armour for a noble. The rear (right)* shows the 'coward's plate' in place over the opening, so called as one should never allow the enemy to see one's back, rendering such an armour piece unnecessary. (Courtesy Tôkyo National Museum)

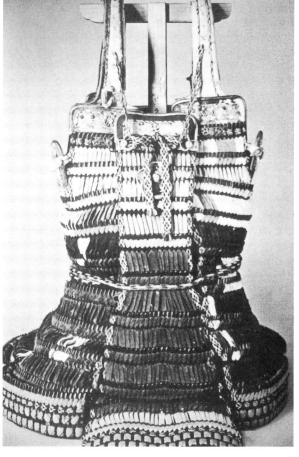

This late-Kamakura/ Nanboku-chô Period dô-maru exhibits an unusual lacing pattern. Note the mittsu kuwagata *and the almost horizontal* shikoro. *(Courtesy Tôkyo National Museum)*

reigns in favour of a son of the other branch. This ignored the fact that the branches would increase in number; and the audacity of openly telling the Emperor what to do was Sadatoki's greatest blunder. He was strong, however, and was able to control the situation; his successors would not be so fortunate. This was one of the factors that would lead to the War of the Northern and Southern Courts in only a few more decades.

Hôjô Takatoki, the last of the *shikken*, had been raised, like many of his contemporaries, in luxury. He spent his time at leisure and left administration to his assistants, who took advantage of the situation. Emperor Go-Daigo, who had mounted the throne in 1318, decided that the time was ripe to overthrow the *bakufu* and restore power to the crown.

Go-Daigo nominated as shôgun Prince Morinaga, his son by a Minamoto daughter, hoping that as Morinaga was head of the temples at Mt. Hiei, the Tendai sect would back his cause; he remembered the fiasco when the monks failed to support Go-Toba, and wanted an ace in his pocket. Takatoki put forth his own candidate, Prince Kazuhito of the rival branch of the Imperial family, and sent troops out to arrest the Emperor. In 1331 Go-Daigo fled the capital, but carried with him the sacred treasures, the Imperial regalia, without which no enthronement could be valid. That did not deter the *shikken*, who put his 18-year-old erstwhile shôgunal candidate on the throne as Emperor Kôgon. Morinaga took up the banner and unleashed war on the Hôjô.

The loyalist forces, led by Kusunoki Masashige, holed up in the fortress of Chihaya. Masashige was a masterful tactician, and played havoc with the Kamakura forces time and again. Once he built a funeral pyre in Chihaya and fooled the *bakufu* commanders into thinking the defenders had all committed suicide. During the confusion he and his forces slipped away; shortly afterwards, the *bakufu* troops abandoned the fortress, and Masashige simply walked back in the main gate, once again in control.

Go-Daigo's forces were able to rally and force Kôgon to flee the capital. Takatoki sent an army under the command of Ashikaga Takauji to Kyôto to put an end to Go-Daigo's ambitions once and for all. When Ashikaga reached the capital and instead proclaimed himself—and Kyôto—for the Emperor, the *shikken* knew he was doomed. Nitta Yoshisada,

That his successors had to follow a man like Tokimune made the contrast all the more painful.

Tokimune was followed by his 14-year-old son Sadatoki, whose first act was to put to death his maternal grandfather and his whole family. He deposed shôgun Prince Koreyasu and installed his own man, Prince Hisa-Akira (brother of the Emperor). He took the tonsure in 1301, but came out of retirement to settle a succession dispute over the Imperial throne. The whole situation was complicated, owing to the simultaneous claims of more than one retired Emperor, all with children. Sadatoki pulled one from the throne and replaced him with a son of the other line (Go-Nijô); and decreed that henceforth Emperors should abdicate after ten-year one of the *bakufu*'s ablest commanders, also turned his coat, and laid siege to Kamakura itself. On 22 May 1333 Takatoki and dozens of his clansmen committed *seppuku*, ritual suicide, ending the Hôjô regency. The Kamakura *bakufu* was over.

The Muromachi *Bakufu* and the Rise of the Two Courts

Go-Daigo, while grateful to the military men who had returned him to power, underestimated their ambitions and their hunger for reward. Yoshisada and Masashige, revered as examples of faith and loyalty, were truly fighting for the Imperial cause, and were more than satisfied with their rewards. Ashikaga Takauji, however, felt that he had been given too little. When an attempt to reform the *bakufu* began in Kamakura and he was sent to quash it, he saw his opportunity. He switched sides again, proclaiming himself for the Hôjô pretender and establishing himself as commander in Kamakura. His intentions were clear to all.

Loyalists rallied again to Go-Daigo's cause, forcing Takauji out of Kamakura, and eventually off the island of Honshû completely. In 1336, however, he returned from Kyûshû at the head of an army. Yoshisada and Masashige planned to retreat and allow him to take Kyôto, and then descend on him from the mountains surrounding the city. The plan was intelligent; but the Emperor and his courtly followers, despite years of living at close quarters with military men, had no understanding of the concept of strategic withdrawal. The duty of soldiers was to fight in battle, and Go-Daigo wanted a battle. Masashige, knowing that the cause was lost, went into battle to lay down his life because his Emperor had commanded it.

At Minatogawa the forces under Yoshisada and Masashige met the combined naval and land power of the Ashikaga. Masashige, surrounded and horribly wounded, committed suicide, and Yoshisada had no choice but to pull back. He lived for two more years, fighting battles in the name of the Emperor, but

finally an arrow found him. It is one of the ironies of Japanese history, in which many of the great houses are linked by ties of blood, that Ashikaga Takauji and Nitta Yoshisada were distant cousins, both descended from Minamoto Yoshiie.

Takauji entered Kyôto and, following the long tradition of puppetmasters, put his own man on the throne. Go-Daigo, retreating to Yoshino south of Kyôto, was still in possession of the regalia, however, so no enthronement could be legitimate. While the new Emperor would be accepted *de facto* as ruler, he could never be valid in the eyes of the gods. Go-Daigo established what came to be called the Nan-chô, or Southern Court, in the mountains of Yoshino in southern Nara, while the Ashikaga-supported line continued to rule what came to be known as the Hoku-chô, or Northern Court.

The Emperor in Kyôto promptly returned the favour of Takauji's support by granting him the title shôgun in 1338. To maintain ties with the Imperial court he moved the offices of the *bakufu* away from Kamakura and back to Kyôto, to a suburb called Muromachi.

There followed nearly six decades of schism during which there were two Emperors, two courts, two sets of Era names, even two sets of aristocracy and honours. It was a situation very similar to that in Christendom when there were two 'Popes', in Rome and Avignon. Both sides had their supporters, who included great families ready and willing to switch allegiance as soon as their interests seemed to dictate it.

Kusunoki Masatsura, son of the late Masashige, took command in the name of the new Southern

This view from the top of a hoshi kabuto shows four plates covered with elaborately sculpted gilt plates; this style, with four 'white sides', was called shihô jiro; usually they took the form of silvered plates. Helmets of six or even eight 'white sides' were also common. (Courtesy Yoroi no Kôzan-dô)

Emperor, Go-Murakami, in 1347. He, too, died in the field against the forces of the new *bakufu*.

Before the lawful Southern Court finally capitulated to the Northern in 1392, a new era would dawn—one which saw major changes in the ways of battle, the military ethics, and the mores of the samurai. The ancient days of loyalty and glory were gone, and individuals and whole clans began changing alliances at the first hint of potential gain. Japan would never be the same again.

EARLY JAPANESE ARMOUR

The nature and style of the armour worn by warriors of the Yayoi Period is unclear. It is likely that it was a variation on that found in the *kôfun* of the 4th–7th centuries; but there are no surviving armours predating the *kôfun*, so there is next to nothing before the mid-4th century for us to study.

Much of what we do know about the design and construction of the earliest armours is due to Suenaga Masao, an armour historian who wrote a masterful and definitive treatise on the subject (*Jôdai no Katchû*, or *Ancient Armour*) before World War II. For the production of the book he also reconstructed virtually every type of armour that had been discovered to date—including all the variations. Almost every writer who has touched on pre-10th-century armours has referred back to Suenaga; and for those with an interest in the old armours, finding a copy of his masterpiece in a second-hand book store is like finding a buried treasure.

The armour that has emerged from the *kôfun* is of two types: tight-fitting solid plate cuirasses called *tankô* (literally 'short shell'), and a skirted cuirass of lamellar construction called *keikô* ('hanging shell'). These are names applied by modern armour historians; their original names are unknown. In the 8th–9th centuries an Imperial edict for the construction of several hundred suits of armour used the term '*kawara*', related to the modern term for 'tile'. Exactly what form of armour the edict referred to is not known, however.

The *tankô* was an hourglass-shaped cuirass, opening up the central front, with hinges of metal or leather on the right and sometimes both sides. The rear rose higher than the front, forming a neat covering for the upper back. The *tankô* had a tight waist, and was obviously individually fitted: some unearthed examples were obviously built for men with more of a paunch than others. It was supported over the shoulders by straps of cotton cloth which, judging by remains, were attached to the *outside* of the armour, rather than a more logical and safe inside fastening.

One of the near-uniform points of consistency on the *tankô* is the design: the plate which rides on the

Glossary

Dô: Cuirass.

Dô-maru: Form of cuirass of scale with attached *kusazuri*, which wraps around the body (hence the name) and ties closed under the right arm.

Fukigaeshi: The 'blow-backs' on the *shikoro* of the helmet.

Gyôyô: Named after apricot leaves, these plates were originally shoulderguards; they also replaced the *sendan* and *kyûbi* on *dô-maru* when worn with *sode*.

Hachiman-za: Another name for the *tehen*.

Haidate: Thigh armour; two styles, one like baggy short pants with plates sewn on and one looking like a split armoured apron, appeared in the early part of the 14th century.

Haramaki-dô: A similar armour to the *dô-maru*, but fastening up the centre back.

Hoshi-kabuto: A helmet marked by the presence of visible, usually large and domed, rivets.

Kabuto: Helmet.

Keikô: An ancient armour of the Kôfun Period, of laced lames of scale. Patterned after continental armours, it was the precursor to all future styles of Japanese armour.

Koshigatana: Companion sword to the *tachi*; essentially a very long knife or a short sword. (It would develop in the 16th century into two weapons: the *wakizashi*, or short sword, and the *tantô*, or dirk.)

Kote: Armoured sleeves.

hips is one of two horizontal bands; there is another at breast level. The remaining plates were usually either triangular, or bands attached to the inside. They could be either riveted in place or attached with leather lacing. Classification of *tankô* found in tombs shows that there does not appear to be any particular correlation by period between those using rivets or leather strapping, nor was there any regional preference between the two, nor between triangular plates and solid lames—all forms were fairly well distri-

These two boards show the inside (top) and outside (bottom) of *sane* construction prior to final lacquering and lacing. They are of rawhide, and have been treated and laced together horizontally and then lacquered several times to make them rigid. The scale construction is mittsume-zane. (From an ô-yoroi *under construction by Toyoda Katsuhiko*)

Kusazuri: Tassets.

Kuwagata: Peculiar twin-horned helmet crest.

Kyûbi-no-ita: A small plate worn on the *ô-yoroi* to protect the left armpit, named for its resemblance to a swallow's tail.

Mabizashi-tsuki kabuto: Influenced by continental styles, this helmet was so called due to the presence of 'baseball cap'-like visor.

Maru-dô: Short-lived hybrid of the *ô-yoroi* and *dô-maru*, with some of the qualities of each.

Men'ôchû: A cloth coat armour of the Nara Period. It seems to have been inspired by continental fashion, and next to nothing is known about its construction.

Mittsume-zane: *Sane* designed with three sets of holes for *odoshi*; thus for treble thickness.

Nagimaki: A polearm best described as a three-foot sword blade attached to a three-foot sword hilt.

Naginata: Halberd.

Nodo-wa: Gorget.

O-arame: A style of *sane* and lacing marked by its great width.

Odoshi: Lacing, whether of leather thong (*kawa-doshi*) or braided, usually silk cord (*ito-odoshi*). Also called *odoshige*, but the latter more literally refers to the material, while *odoshi* could also refer to pattern, colour, and style.

O-yoroi: Great armour; three large *kusazuri* pendant from a nearly square cuirass and the fourth separate, attached to a side plate.

Sane (also *kozane*): Scales; the basic components of a suit of Japanese armour.

Se-ita: Piece of armour resembling a very long *kusazuri* designed to protect the opening of the *haramaki*.

Sendan-no-ita: A small plate resembling a small *sode* worn on the *ô-yoroi* to protect the right armpit.

Shikoro: Lames to protect the nape of the neck.

Shôkakufû kabuto (also *shôkaku-tsuki*): Ancient form of helmet; so-called due to the apparent 'battering ram' at the visor.

Sode: Pauldrons, shoulder/upper arm armour.

Sô-men: Full face mask; rarely used.

Suneate: Shin guards.

Tachi: Sword.

Tankô: An ancient armour of the Kôfun Period with a solidly riveted or laced cuirass.

Tehen: The ornamental opening at the top of a helmet.

Tsuji-kabuto: A helmet with no visible rivets, the edges of the plates having been turned up.

Tsurubashiri: The printed leather 'bib' on the front of the *ô-yoroi*, to allow the bowstring smooth passage across the scales.

Watagami: Shoulder straps.

Yari: Spear.

The ô-yoroi was a
beautiful piece of art as
well as a defensive item of
dress. This modern
reconstruction of a

Kamakura armour is
typical of the more
utilitarian type, boasting a
minimum of decoration.

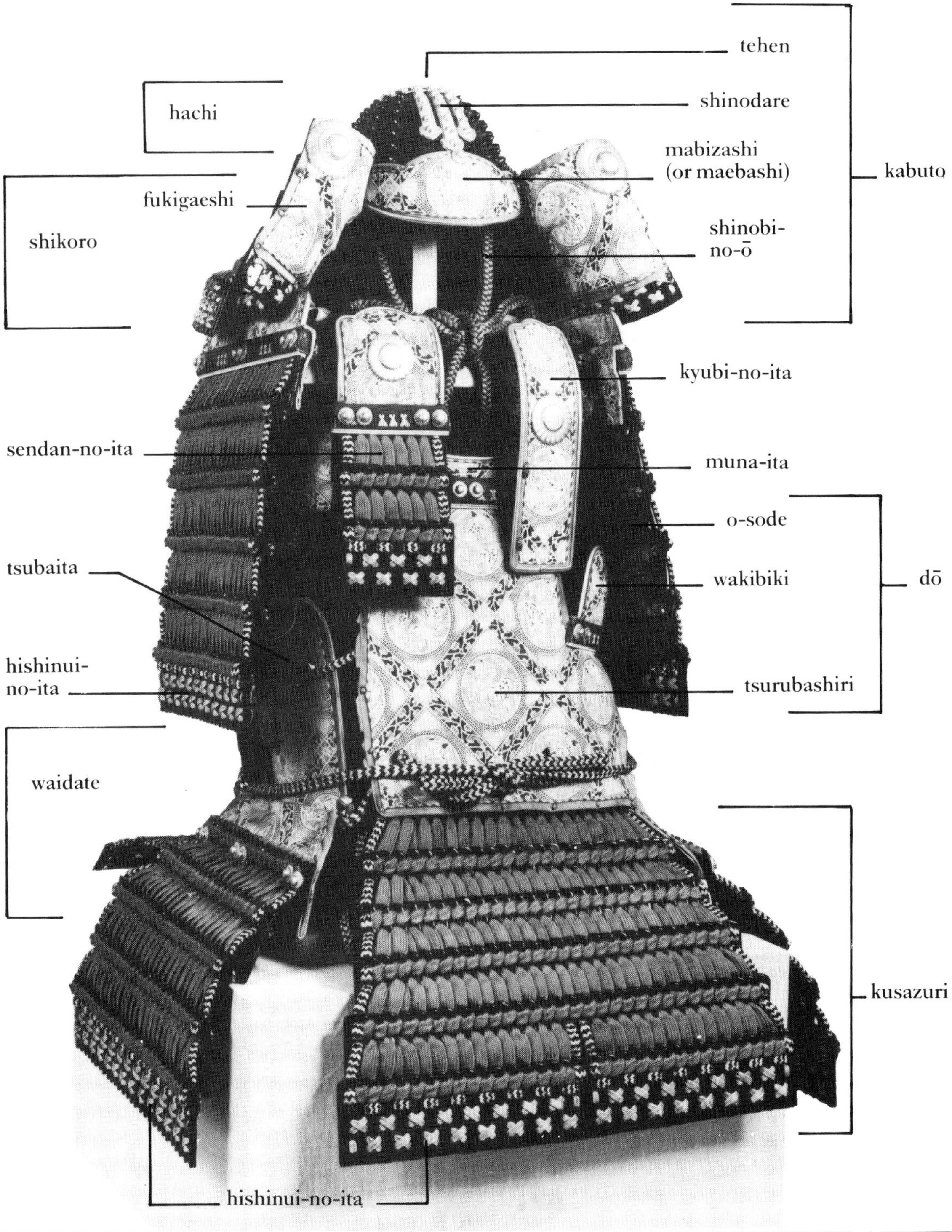

tehen

shinodare

mabizashi
(or maebashi)

shinobi-
no-ō

kabuto

hachi

fukigaeshi

shikoro

kyubi-no-ita

sendan-no-ita

muna-ita

o-sode

wakibiki

dō

tsubaita

hishinui-
no-ita

tsurubashiri

waidate

kusazuri

hishinui-no-ita

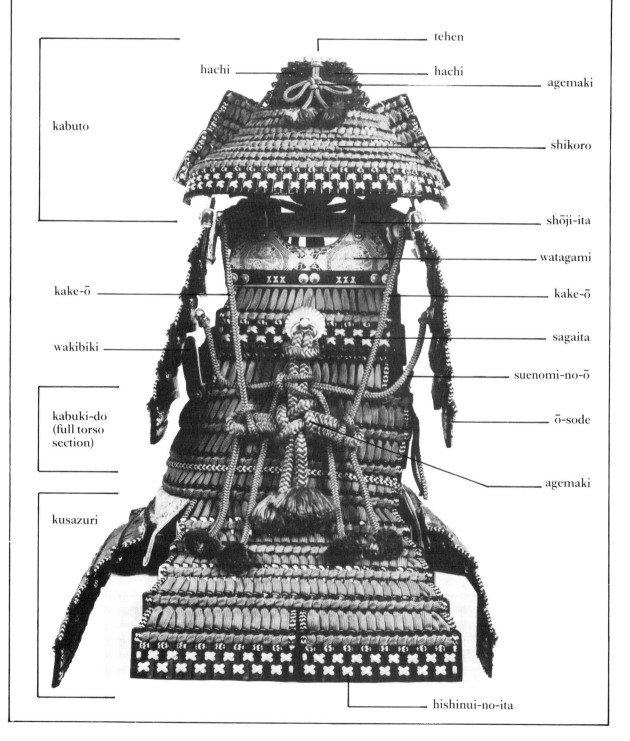

All of the parts are here identified. The back displays the complex pattern of cords which assured that the sode would sit properly.

Sometimes, to save time, the warriors would leave all the cords tied, and just slide into the armour. (Courtesy Tôkyo National Museum)

tehen

hachi — — hachi

agemaki

kabuto

shikoro

shōji-ita

watagami

kake-ō — — kake-ō

sagaita

wakibiki

suenomi-no-ō

ō-sode

kabuki-do (full torso section)

agemaki

kusazuri

hishinui-no-ita

buted throughout the period and over the various tumuli.

The likely origin of the *tankô* (though there is scant archaeological evidence) is that it originated as a leather or perhaps even wooden armour, held together by leather cords, and when it made the shift to metal the cord method of attachment was in some cases kept. There are several preserved fragments of what has been identified as a *tankô*-like cuirass made of wood dated to around the late 1st or 2nd century. As it is the only existing survivor it is not clear how

common they were, but it is likely that they were far from rare.

At some point, possibly early in the 4th century or in the late 3rd, a huge, knee-length bell-shaped skirt defence made its appearance. This skirt section, comparable to a greatly elongated fauld, was usually made of lames, and loosely laced for flexibility. The few surviving examples are of metal. Considering that most *haniwa* depicting the *tankô* show such a skirt, it is odd that so few have ever been found; and it may be that many were made of leather, and have rotted away.

Not all of the skirts were fashioned of laced lames, if one is to go by the *haniwa* evidence. The depictions of the *tankô* proper are generally quite accurate, so it is likely that their depictions of the skirt were, as well. Some would seem to have repeated the triangular pattern on the lames, but in what form we can only speculate. Armour historian Sasama Yoshihiko has designed some reconstructions which allow for the leather panels to be applied to the surface in lieu of lacing (see Plate B)—a logical conclusion. The few cases where the skirt section has survived in tumuli indicate that most were attached to the bottom of a separate cuirass using the bell-lip of the cuirass's base, although a few were actually laced or buckled into place. There were usually front and back sections, regardless of form or execution.

In addition to the skirt, there is a separate gorget-like section which was attached to a pair of multi-lame shoulder guards. In design and execution they were not unlike the upper parts of the Roman legionaries' *lorica segmentata*.

Helmets

The helmet generally depicted with the *tankô* is called (today) *shôkakufû kabuto* or *shôkaku-tsuki kabuto*, meaning 'attached battering-ram helmet'. The reference to its shape, with a protruding pointed brow section, is obvious; it looks like an upturned boat. It, like the *tankô*, consists of horizontal wrapping lames, with small triangular or rectangular

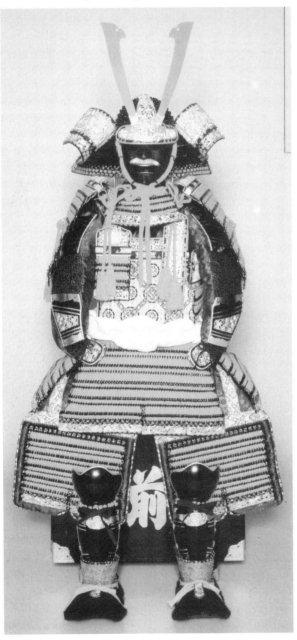

This is an example of the more ornate style, and even this could be considered sedate compared to some of the 'parade' armours donated to shrines during the Kamakura Period. The presence of haidate, *the apron-like thigh guards, is an Edo Period (1600–1868) affectation. (Courtesy* Yoroi no Kôzan-dô)

Himiko's Yamataikoku, c. 230
1: Himiko
2: Yayoi military officer
3: Yayoi common soldier

A

Invasion of Korea, 366
1: Jingû Kôgô
2: Common warrior
3: Commander
4: Servant

B

Mononobe's chastisement of Iwai, 527
1: Yamato Mononofu
2: Mononobe no Arakabi
3: Iwai
4: Mononobe clansman

C

Jinshin no Ran, 672
1: Ōama, the future Emperor Tenmu
2: Ōtomo no Makuta
3: Ōtomo no Fukei

D

Naramaro's Revolt, 757
1: Tachibana Naramaro
2: Warrior from Nakamaro's house
3: Nakamaro's lieutenant

Tenkei no Ran, 940
1: Taira no Masakado
2: Taira clan bushi

F

Heian fashions, 1083
1: Courtier in formal dress
2: Palace guard, duty uniform
3: Noble in daytime costume
4: Court lady in formal attire

G

H

Go-Sannen no Eki, 1086
1: Minamoto no Yoshiie
2: Warrior monk
3: Minamoto samurai

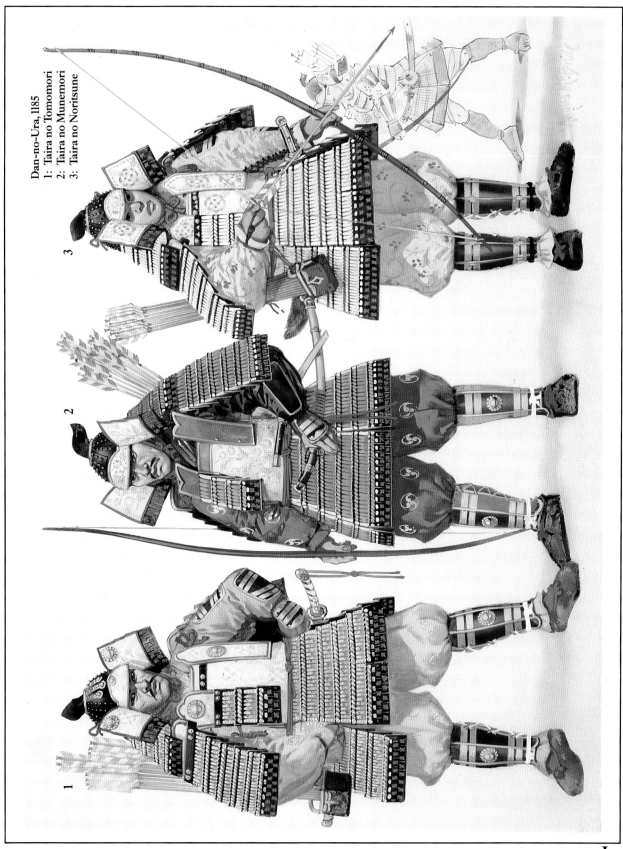

Dan-no-Ura, 1185
1: Taira no Tomomori
2: Taira no Munemori
3: Taira no Noritsune

1

2

3

I

Shokyû no Ran, 1221
1: Hôjô samurai
2: Hôjô Yasutoki
3: Hôjô retainer

AngusMcBride

J

The Mongol invasion, 1181
1: Shôni no Kagesuke
2: Ashigaru
3: Kyûshû samurai

Nanboku-chô, c. 1333
1: Ashikaga Takauji
2: Nitta Yoshisada
3: Kusunoki Masashige
4: Samurai retainer

L

plates laced or riveted in, though models with solid plates have also been found. Most often, the helmet had pendant lames suspended by leather thongs to protect the nape of the neck. This was called the *shikoro*. Some helmets had one broad *shikoro* lame, some several narrow ones; again, like the execution of the plates, there was no uniformity. Many such helmets were also fitted with a crest holder on top which held pheasant tail feathers.

From the 5th century a rounder form of helmet called *mabizashi-tsuke kabuto* ('visor-attached helmet'), with a 'baseball cap' flat visor, was also worn with the *tankô*. This was an imported style, modelled after the helmets of the Korean and Chinese warriors encountered on the continent. Such helmets were made *en suite* with the later lamellar armours, but examples have been found in the same tombs as *tankô*. Most had a cup-shaped crest holder supported by a bronze tube, presumably for some sort of plume.

Many *haniwa* show helmets with cheek-pieces separate from the rest of the *shikoro*. No such finds have yet been made, but it is not unlikely that they existed.

The last pieces of armour were for the forearms and shins. Very few have survived unscathed, but enough have to give us some ideas as to their construction. There were generally two types: those formed like tubes, of one or two semi-circular plates, and those made of splints. Usually attached to the forearm guards were flat metal plates or a lamellar defence for the back of the hand.

One of the many frustrations of armour archaeology in Japan is that full suits have seldom been unearthed: some tombs had only a cuirass, some only a helmet, some several of either. The few that held enough to make an 'entire suit' usually had many different parts, in such a state that there is no certainty as to which ones constituted the suit. (One tomb, containing no armour, did contain over 3,000 iron swords alone.) Often all there is to go on is the pattern of construction, and even there no great consistency existed.

Scale Armour

The *keikô*—scale armour—was doubtless inspired by battle gear worn on the continent. The Koreans and the Chinese had been using lamellar armours for hundreds of years, and such armours were perfectly

The Tate-nashi no Yoroi ('Armour With No Shield') was a Takeda Clan heirloom. The lacing pattern of cherry blossoms printed on leather is called kozakura odoshi. *No one is sure when this armour was* made, but it is Heian Period in style; one of the fabled suits of Genji armour was called Tate-nashi, *and the Takeda were a branch of the Minamoto clan. (Courtesy Kanda Jinja)*

suited to the mounted warfare practised on the continent. The Yamato warriors, on the other hand, had always fought on foot; horses were not indigenous to the Japanese archipelago. At some point during one of their many early incursions into Korea they were presumably struck by the horse's usefulness in combat, and doubtless found that the flexible scale armour of the Koreans was better suited to mounted combat than the solid *tankô*.

At what date this occurred is unknown, but horses were introduced to Japan sometime around the early 5th century, perhaps as early as the 4th (it is in the 5th century that horse furniture first became a part of tomb 'offerings'); but the lamellar armours came later. It was sometime in the late 5th century that the *keikô* made its appearance in Japan, in a manner slightly modified from the Korean models—it resembled, at least in silhouette, the skirted *tankô*.

The variety of size and style of sane *is clear in this photograph. The bottom scales are* mittsume-zane, *and the two on the top right are* ô-arame. *The one on the far left is 'typical' Kamakura/Nanboku-chô Period size. (From reconstructions by Morita, in the possession of Orikasa Teruo)*

The *keikô* wrapped around the wearer's body and was fastened up the front with ties. At first there were two types, both made up of 'steps' of scales laced horizontally together into boards; one kind was held together with leather straps running down the outside of the steps, and the other with a more conventional under-over lacing of braided cord or leather. The shoulder straps were again of cotton cloth, tied over the points of the shoulder. This actually gave the name to future shoulder straps on armour—*watagami*, or cotton shoulders—even when made of leather or metal.

A distinctive variation of the *keikô* appeared in the 7th or 8th century. It looked something like a modern poncho, and had no integral side protection. Exactly how this style of armour evolved is not clear; it is possible that it had something to do with ease of wear, although the conventional *keikô* could not have been much more difficult to put on than a coat. The new style even required the wearer to don the side plates first (however they were attached and worn) and then the armour proper.

For a while the *tankô* held its own against the *keikô*,

but the popularity of scale armour began to predominate in the 6th and 7th centuries. There were a few interesting 'half-breeds', notably a *tankô* made with a removable skirt of large scales.

Be it metal or leather, most Japanese armour was lacquered, even from the earliest days; Japan is a humid country, and lacquering would be necessary for the preservation of the armour. It may be that one reason some armour pieces have not been discovered is that they were not lacquered, and were perhaps of leather. Some pieces, especially those for men of considerable rank, were gilded.

One of the most troublesome Japanese armours for the historian is the *men'ôchû*, literally 'cotton coat armour', which appeared only briefly during the late Asuka and early Nara Periods. In style and construction it seems to have nothing in common with either of the two indigenous armours, the *tankô* or the *keikô*. It is, however, apparently virtually identical to an armour seen in occasional contemporary Chinese statuary and illustrations. Considering that the 6th and 7th centuries, the time of the appearance of the *men'ôchû*, coincide with the greatest influx of Chinese learning and culture, it is probable that this accounts for its appearance on the Japanese scene.

We are uncertain as to the actual construction of the suit: we know its form, but not how it was made. Some have speculated that it was actually some form of jazerant-work, of metal or leather plates riveted or sewn directly to the outside of a cloth coat and cap; others speculate that the *men'ôchû* was a brigandine, with plates under or sandwiched between layers of cloth. Either or both would be possible, as armours of similar overall design and both modes of construction exist as Chinese examples (e.g., China's *k'ai*, the former, and *k'ai i*, the latter). As not a single one from Japan survives in any form or condition it is quite possible that the armour was simply a heavily padded coat of multiple layers made to the Chinese pattern. (In fact, such may have also existed in China.) This armour did not last long; by the time the capital had moved to Heian (Kyôto), it was long gone.

Concurrent with the short-lived *men'ôchû*, the development and construction of scale armours naturally continued. One form of cuirass which evolved was a descendant of the wrap-around *keikô*. The opening was moved to under the right arm; perhaps this was a development concurrent with the *ô-yoroi*, which also had its opening on the right side.

It is easy to see how the conversion to the *ô-yoroi* (literally, 'great armour') came about: simplicity of wear was important. Armour designers left a single side (under the right arm) open, to be defended by a separate plate, and made the rest of the armour rigidly horseshoe-shaped, so that it wraps around the wearer and overlaps the defending side plate.

Scales and Lacing

When the *ô-yoroi* appeared, there was a change in the scales, or *kozane*, making up the box-like armour. Previously they had been individually lacquered, then laced together; this provided a certain amount of flexibility. With the advent of the new armour style, the *kozane* were first formed into long boards and only then lacquered, rendering the boards rigid. It was more protective, both against the elements and the enemy, but the wearer suffered from a slight loss of mobility.

Armours were made of *kozane* of metal or leather, and frequently of both: many suits were made predominantly of leather scales with large concentrations of metal scales, or alternations of metal and leather in areas most likely to take stress or damage. The same suit of armour would also often have several different sizes of *sane*. Those for the *shikoro* would require a taper; those for the *sode* were usually shorter; often those of the *kusazuri* and the trunk section would be different as well.

One generalisation that holds fairly true is that as the years passed the size of *sane* shrunk. Scales on some old *ô-yoroi*—12th century and earlier—were huge: two and three inches across. This style of scale was called *ô-arame*, and is one of the trademarks of ancient armours.

Another scale anomaly considered to be a mark of antiquity—though erroneously—is *mittsume-zane*, three-eyed scales, so called for their extra width and third set of eyes or holes for lacing. Each *sane* was designed to overlap half of the *sane* to its left, and to be overlapped half-way by the one on its right. *Mittsume-zane* had a triple overlap, creating a triple thickness of scale. The reason for its appearance may

have been simple economy. Rawhide thick enough and of the right quality for *sane* was hard to come by, as only part of a hide could be used. Rather than have any wastage, if the scales were triple thickness instead of double, all the leather could be used. Most *mittsume-zane* are indeed old, but they are not the oldest.

Through all these developments and mutations there was one constant. *Sane* had a series of four holes (two sets for regular *sane*, three for *mittsume-zane*) in the lower half for the binding lacing, which held the rows of scales together in lames; and a series of three holes—usually slightly larger to accommodate the broader lacing—on the top half for the suspensory

This ô-yoroi exhibits a rather liberal use of the crest of the wearer. The overall style is Kamakura, but the decoration—and the haidate—*are definitely Edo in flavour. (Courtesy* Yoroi no Kôzan-dô)

現代

lacing. The bottom lame of any piece of armour was invariably laced with bright silk or leather—red or orange being the most common colours—to produce a more showy effect.

The suspensory lacing, of dyed leather strips or brightly coloured silk twill threads braided into flat, broad cord, was what lent the armour its dashing appearance. Cuirasses are identified first by the lacing pattern or colour and then by the actual style of the armour. It is only natural that the term for the lacing, *odoshi* or *odoshige*, comes from the verb *odosu*, 'to intimidate'. (The '*-ge*' is from the word for hair.)

Some armour historians of bygone days have tried applying motives and meanings to lacing patterns and

colours, much in the same way as Victorian and earlier heraldists tried to convince people that *argent* meant virtue, *azure* meant chastity, *gules* meant loyalty, and so on. To the Japanese warrior of the historic age such a theory would be laughable. The wealthier ones had several suits, and wore whatever was convenient or suited their fancy on any given day.

The Ô-Yoroi

The ô-yoroi is probably the armour people think of first when they think of samurai. It is a boxy-looking armour, odd to Western eyes accustomed to body-shaped iron plates, yet it does what it was designed to do with remarkable efficiency. It was, first and last, armour for the mounted warrior. When the ô-yoroi 'great armour' first appeared warriors of rank fought from horseback, and the weapon of choice was the deadly longbow.

The main body of the armour is horseshoe-shaped, and rigidly protects the trunk by encasing it in four steps of lames, with an additional two boards protecting the chest, and two more for the back. Pendant from it at the front, left side, and back are three large tassets called *kusazuri* which reach to mid-thigh, with rigidly lacquered lames floating loosely on their rows of suspensory braid. The right side of the torso is defended by a solid metal plate called the *waidate*, from which is suspended the fourth *kusazuri*.

The front of the torso section is covered with a printed leather panel called a *tsurubashiri* ('bowstring running'). Its purpose is to protect both scales and bowstring from each other—the bowstring from snagging, the scales from wear and tear. With the huge bows and wide-brimmed helmets of the samurai, the bow was often drawn to and released from the chest area, not the cheek. The designs used for the *tsurubashiri* ranged from geometrical patterns to illustrations of Shinto and Buddhist deities, dragons, and floral patterns. Whatever design was used here was repeated throughout the rest of the

The dô-maru, though simpler than the ô-yoroi, need not be any less ornate, as this example shows. The lacing pattern, called omodaka, is of white, green, and purple on an orange base. The kote are 16th century in style, and this pattern of haidate never existed, but other than that it is a good reconstruction of a Kamakura dô-maru. Note the unusual presence of sendan-no-ita and kyûbi-no-ita. (Courtesy Yoroi no Kôzan-dô) armour wherever leather panels were used (notably the turnbacks on the *shikoro*, the *waidate*, and covering for the top plates of all the scales).

Also part of the *ô-yoroi* were a pair of large flat shoulder guards called *sode* (literally 'sleeve'). Their design makes them almost resemble squared off *kusazuri*. A series of cords running off the top of the *sode* attached it to the *watagami* (shoulder strap), while another cord coming off the back attached to the *agemaki* bow on the back of the armour, anchoring it in place. The *sode* were made large specifically because the mounted warrior could not handle a bow, control his mount, and hold a shield all at the same time.

Hanging from the top of the breastplate in front of the armpits were two asymmetrical plates called the *sendan no ita* and *kyûbi no ita*. The *sendan* resembles a small *sode*, and the *kyûbi* is a long, narrow, solid plate. They were designed to protect the armpit area when the arms were in motion.

The *Dô-Maru* and the *Haramaki-dô*

The *dô-maru* (literally 'torso round') was a tighter fitting armour than the *ô-yoroi*, but also fastened under the right arm. However, it met and even overlapped slightly, calling for no extra plates like the *waidate*. It also had more *kusazuri* tassets, generally seven. The *dô-maru* had no leather *tsurubashiri* chest panel either, though in the late 12th century there was a short-lived bastard of the *ô-yoroi* and *dô-maru* called the *dô-maru yoroi* which had both the large number of tassets and the *tsurubashiri*.

The *dô-maru* appeared early — during the Nara Era and well before the *ô-yoroi* — but in its earliest incarnations was still considered a variation of the *keikô*. It had the benefit of being lighter than other armours, and since it fitted closer to the body was easier to move and fight in. It was a plainer armour, and as such was deemed unsuitable for warriors of rank; but at about the time of the Genpei War even upper class samurai began wearing it occasionally, in deference to its ease of wear and comfort.

Almost identical in style to the *dô-maru* was the *haramaki-dô* (literally 'belly-wrap torso'). The only difference was that the closure was up the back, and rather than an overlap there was actually a gap; a separate piece, looking like a section of the cuirass with a single *kusazuri*, was often worn to cover this

This halberdier wears a dô-maru of graded blue lacing (kon susogu odoshi). Note that even in motion sode, when properly tied down, do not leave the arm unprotected. Note also the rigidity of the slinging of the sword, and the way that the arrows jut out. This is a very accurate example of the gear in action.

opening. It was called *se-ita* ('back plate'); but as one should never show the enemy one's back, and therefore should not need such a plate, it was frequently called a 'coward's plate'. This style of armour appeared fairly late, perhaps around the 12th century.

When worn by retainers, the huge *sode* used with *ô-yoroi* were not part of the *dô-maru/haramaki* set. Rather, two plates were hung off the shoulder straps over the edge of the shoulders. These were shaped roughly — at least originally — like apricot leaves, hence their name, *gyôyô*. When the *dô-maru* or *haramaki* was worn by men of rank they would often wear the *sode* with them, repositioning the *gyôyô* to hang in front of the armpits as replacements for the *sendan* and *kyûbi no ita*.

The Helmet

The *kabuto*, or helmet, was made en suite with the armour, be it *ô-yoroi*, *dô-maru*, or *haramaki*. The

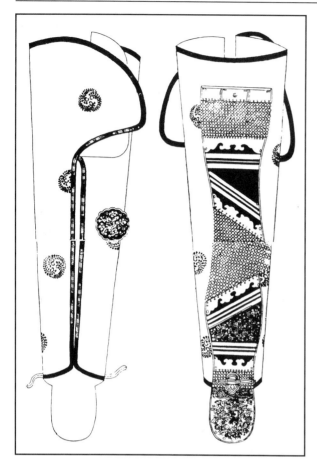

In Nara's Kasuga Taisha are a pair of ornate kote *said to have been owned by Minamoto no Yoshitsune.*

Here they are as depicted in Arai Hakuseki's historical armour treatise, Honchô Gunkikô.

concept of 'en suite' when discussing Japanese armour almost invariably comes down to lacing pattern. Scale type is also a factor; no matter what the style of *odoshi*, if the *shikoro* were *kozane* and the *dô* were *ô-arame*, it would look distinctly odd.

The earliest *kabuto* worn with *ô-yoroi* were distantly related to both the *shôkakufû* and *mabizashi-tsuki kabuto*, being a kind of half-and-half of each. They generally had only a few plates, ten to 12 being common. (This is in contrast to the 'age of battles'—the Sengoku Era of 1550–1600—when helmets of 32, 62 and 72 plates were far from uncommon, and many *daimyô* owned 120-plate *kabuto*.)

The *shikoro* on these *kabuto* was angled almost straight down at first, but towards the 13th century began widening; it reached its extreme point in the 1330s during the early phase of the Nanboku-chô conflict, when it was almost vertically extended, looking like an open umbrella. In fact, it received the name *kasa-jikoro* ('umbrella *shikoro*') for this shape.

One of the characteristics of the *kabuto* is the presence of huge *fukigaeshi* (blow-backs) spreading out and back like wings from the front of the *shikoro*. The purpose was probably to prevent a downward sword-stroke from severing the *odoshi*.

Because of the *shikoro*, *kabuto* were often back-heavy, making careful tying of the helmet cords necessary. Many clans even had their own 'secret methods' of doing so.

Although helmets of many elaborate designs—grotesques—appeared during the Sengoku Period, until the 15th century *kabuto* were exclusively of the multiplate variety, which means that when viewed from above they present a pattern of radial segments. At the crown of the *kabuto*, the centre where all the plates come together, is an ornamental (often gilt) doughnut-shaped plate. The purpose of this piece, called alternatively *tehen* or *Hachiman-za*, has been explained by many different rationales. Favourites include: being an opening to the heavens to allow the spirit of the war god Hachiman (*Hachiman-za* means 'seat of Hachiman') to enter the warrior; to allow air out so the samurai would not float when trying to hide in water (which makes one wonder why he would do so); and to allow the samurai's topknot to pass through the helmet. While the hole was certainly used for the latter purpose, that can hardly be the reason for the *tehen*; its true origin is probably simply that the armourer wanted to avoid the technical difficulty of joining many plates together at a single point.

The multiplate helmets were held together with rivets. There were two types: rivets which had been filed down and lacquered over, and those which were huge, bulbous affairs. *Kabuto* with large rivets are called *hoshi* ('star') *kabuto*, and those without are called *tsuji* ('ribbed') *kabuto*. The latter name was applied due to the ridges on the edges of the plates, which were turned up.

Occasionally a crest called a *kuwagata* would be attached to the front of the helmet. The shape and size changed through the years, but they were almost invariably signs of rank; not everyone could wear them. The crest holders were frequently highly ornamental.

Other Armour

For arm protection, *kote* ('basket sleeves') were worn from the earliest days, but the forms changed greatly. During the early Heian Period modern style *kote* first appeared. They resembled bags, and were more useful for tucking the huge sleeves of the armour robe out of the way of the bowstring than as a defence: indeed, plates were apparently attached to some only as an afterthought. For hundreds of years only the left one was worn, emphasising its role as an archer's accessory rather than as a practical piece of armour. It was not until the Genpei War, when hand to hand combat began to occur with regularity, that wearing a pair became common.

There were two types: those sewn closed (essentially a long open-ended bag), and those which were laced up along the bottom of the arm. The plates were generally four in number: a piece for the back of the hand, one for the forearm, one for the upper arm, and a small circular plate on the elbow. They were often very ornamental when owned by the upper classes, in which case they were made en suite with the *suneate* (shin guard).

The shin was the most protected part of the leg; as far back as the early Kôfun Era, and perhaps before, splint shin guards were in use. Early Heian *suneate* had no plates to protect the knee, but later ones had risers that protected the knee and sometimes a good deal of the thigh as well.

A split apron-like thigh defence called the *haidate* appeared (actually a reappearance of thigh armour) at the very end of the Kamakura shôgunate. A style resembling baggy shorts with plates sewn onto the front also appeared at about this time, but this style was to be rare in the future.

The final pieces of armour were designed for the face and neck. A throat guard called a *nodo-wa* was commonly worn under the *ô-yoroi*, covering the only part of the torso unprotected. A face mask called a *sô-men* was occasionally used, though not popularly, as it was rather uncomfortable and restricted breathing and vision.

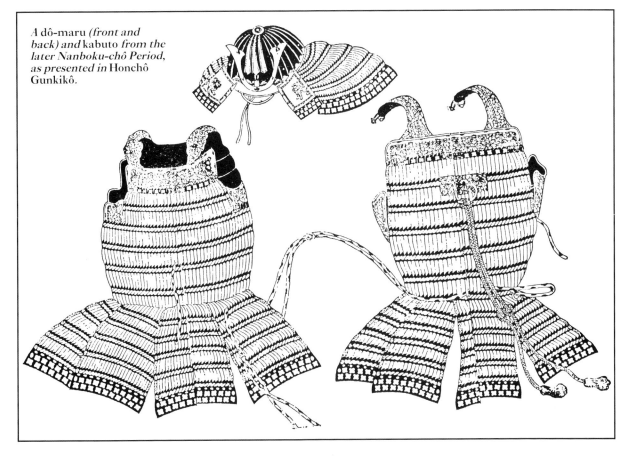

A dô-maru (front and back) and kabuto from the later Nanboku-chô Period, as presented in Honchô Gunkikô.

THE PLATES

Plate A: Himiko's Yamataikoku, c. 230

All we know of Himiko and her proto-empire is what the Wei chroniclers tell us. Oddly, domestic histories are silent on her, her 28-clan confederation, and her warfare with neighbours.

A1: Himiko

The priestess/queen was never seen in public after assuming power, but a few people had access to her, including her co-ruler brother. This costume is that depicted for her in almost all texts, and is based on accounts in the Wei Chronicles and archaeological findings. Around her neck she wears the beads that are almost universal among members of the later Yayoi/Yamato society. One of the Three Sacred Treasures of the Japanese Imperial House is a set of such beads, ancient in lineage. (Source: Japan Costume Museum)

A2: Yayoi military officer

The cuirass section of the *tankô* was apparently the earliest indigenous armour. Although no suits remain, there are a few fragments of one such cuirass which are enough to give an indication of their style. They were made of carved hardwood, and coated with russet, red, and black pigmented lacquers. The shield is typical of the early period, and the spiral boss is characteristic; they have been found even in the southern Korean peninsula (the region that was ancient Mimana). The polearm is a common type of halberd. The simple all-in-one sword had a hilt wrapped with leather, and the ring section held a lanyard for attaching it to the wrist. (Reconstruction by the author)

A3: Yayoi common soldier

Likely armour for most was a simple wooden cuirass. The unusual polearm the warrior carries had been phased out by the 300s, but several of these blades have been unearthed. They were used like a pickaxe,

This reproduction from the Honchô Gunkikô *shows an armour said to have belonged to Minamoto no Yoshitsune. It seems to be along the pattern of* dô-maru, *but has* kusazuri *like an ô-yoroi. Note the* sendan-no-ita *and* kyûbi-no-ita. *The* kabuto *is fairly famous and popularly considered authentically to have been his. The armour was lost in a fire in the 19th century.*

An elaborate kabuto *in Nara's Kôfuku-ji from the latter part of the Nanboku-chô Period, reproduced in the* Honchô Gunkikô. *The elaborately sculpted trees and flowers are of thick gilt brass.*

and are similar to weapons used in China during the period 500–200 BC. The unusual short sword, similar to one found at Yoshinogari, is believed to have been used point down, with stabbing motions. (Reconstruction by the author)

Plate B: Invasion of Korea, 366

It is certain that the empress-regent *Jingû Kôgô* did not in fact attack Korea shortly before 200 as written in the *Kojiki*, but in the 4th century. She invaded Silla, forcing the king to submit, and extracted from him an oath to send annual tributes of 80 boats laden with gold, silver, cloth, and other valuables. As Japanese excursions into Korea went, this one was rather successful.

B1: Jingû Kôgô

According to legend the widow of the Emperor Kaika was pregnant when she made the crossing to Korea, tying a stone to her belly and vowing not to give birth until she had finished the campaign. The son became the Emperor Ôjin, later deified and revered as Hachiman, the god of war and the Minamoto clan tutelary deity. A likely explanation for the story is to explain how a child who was to become Emperor was born years after the death of his father, the previous Emperor. Jingû is shown here wearing a *tankô* typical of the time, but with the addition of a protective skirt. Though frequently depicted on *haniwa*, no such skirt survives and so its existence is speculative. She wears *magatama* beads. (Source: the *tankô* is from Usui-ikenzaki Kôfun, and the skirt is based on a *haniwa* depicting an identical cuirass from the Shiraishi Fukuyama Kôfun, Gunma Pref.)

B2: Common warrior

This warrior wears a *tankô* of unusual form: vertical plates laced together, opening up the left side, not wholly unlike the armour style of 1,200 years later. Only two such armours have been discovered so far, but this seems to be an old form of *tankô*, and it is likely that many were originally of the same pattern.

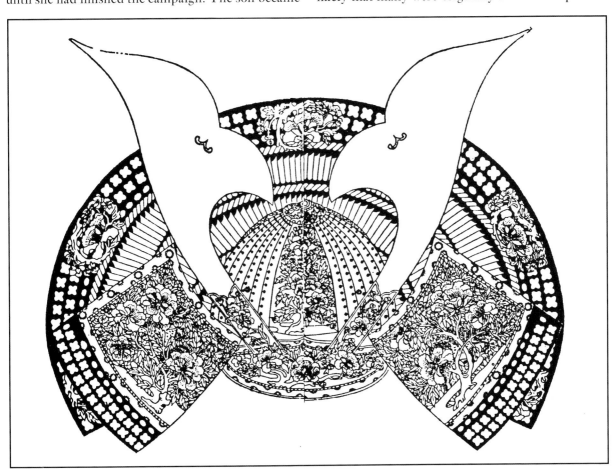

He wears his hair in the typical Yamato style, and his clothing seems to have been almost uniform within that culture; the long, baggy pants tied up at the knee are seen in most anthropomorphic *haniwa*. Several such shields have been found. (Source: a *tankô* recovered from the Sôguchi Kôfun, Yamanashi Pref.)

B3: Commander
This warrior also wears a *tankô* of unusual form, with a built-in standing collar at the back and protective wings. Only a few have been recovered showing this aberration. It is possible that this is actually a later period model, but dating at this point is inaccurate. A heavy, short-bladed sword of similar style is preserved in the Shôsoin, and reproduced in Kasuga Jinja, Nara.

B4: Servant
The civilian fashions of ancient Japan seem to have shown very little variation from place to place or over several centuries. Most of what is known about them comes from examination of *haniwa*. This man is shown wearing the typical attire, complete with *magatama* beads. The garb worn under armour was probably identical. (Source: a model in the Japan Costume Museum)

Plate C: Mononobe's chastisement of Iwai, 527
Iwai, the governor of Tsukushi on northern Kyûshû, entered into a treasonable alliance with the king of Silla, blocking Yamato attempts to send relief to Mimana. This was the first rebellion against the Yamato Sun Line. Mononobe no Arakabi was sent to put an end to the satrap's insurrection. In 528 Iwai was overthrown, and the virtual autonomy which his region had long enjoyed ended with the establishment of Dazaifu, the central government's military base of operations in Kyûshû.

C1: Yamato Mononofu
The shoulder guards as seen here have been found in only a few excavated tombs, but may have been in more common use judging by their appearance on several *haniwa*. The shoulder protector consists of several narrow metal lames which are suspended by leather strapping. The whole affair is very much like the Roman legionary's shoulder armour on the *lorica segmentata*. It is not known whether the skirt plates were worn while mounted, which would seem uncomfortable and inconvenient. The horse furniture here is consistent with that used throughout the Kôfun Period. (Source: an armour from the Tannowa Nishi Koyama-Ryô Kôfun, Ôsaka)

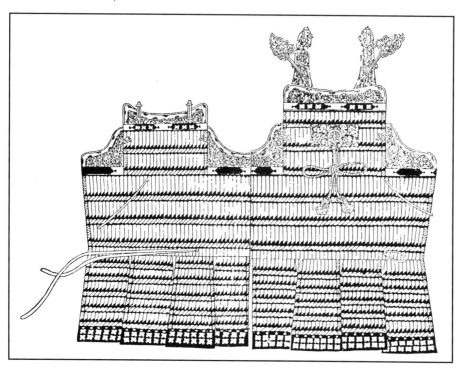

The dô-maru laid out flat in the Honchô Gunkikô to show the details of its construction, the gyôyô set to protect the shoulders. Note that it would be impossible to lay an ô-yoroi out flat like this without destroying the integrity of the lacquering.

C2: Mononobe no Arakabi

Arakabi had earlier feigned an illness to avoid having to go to Korea (as he felt that his mission to turn over parts of Mimana to Paekche was an insult to Japan); but when the call came from the Emperor to destroy Iwai and send troops to Mimana he went readily. This depiction is of Arakabi in a complete suit of *tankô* armour; it includes forearm guards, a gorget of sorts, and a lamellar skirt. The shin guards are missing. It is an excellent example of the state-of-the-art for the *tankô*, and perhaps shows why it was phased out in favour of the *keikô*. The unusual beak of the helmet makes Arakabi look like some armoured parrot; this was the most extreme form of the *shukakufû kabuto*. (Source: combined from finds in the Obitoki Enshô-ji Tsukayama #1 Kôfun and the Kumonobe Kurumazuka Kôfun, Nara)

C3: Iwai

Not much is known about Iwai beyond the fact that he was in league with Korean forces and that he rebelled against the Yamato court. He was a fairly powerful man, however, ruling his domain in northern Kyûshû like an absolute monarch. This depiction shows that the *keikô*, like the *tankô*, could easily be rendered unwieldy. While many *haniwa* show such fully-suited individuals, only one relatively 'complete' suit has ever been discovered, and that was in pieces. The leg defences, made of two sections (thigh and calf), are simply wrapped around the leg and tied closed in the back. What methods of suspension were used is unknown. It is hard to believe such a monstrosity could have been worn in actual combat with any frequency. Could it have been a sort of parade armour? (Source: an armour from the Minowa Ama no Miya Kôfun, Gunma Pref.)

C4: Mononobe clansman

One of the most complete and best preserved *keikô* ever discovered was from the Nagamochiyama Kôfun. Due to damage incurred over the years it is no longer in its original state of preservation, but ample studies were made, and photographs allow its reconstruction here. It is believed to be typical of those worn by the upper class. The cuirass style here seems to be the most common form of *keikô*. It is almost identical in cut and scale type to that of Iwai, but here the lacing ran through the scales; another variation

(e.g. the Tenguyama Kôfun *keikô*) has the torso laced with running thong and the skirt laced with thong overlaid.

D: Jinshin no Ran, 672

Ôama, third son of Emperor Jomei (d. 641), was chosen as heir to his brother, Tenji. Upon Tenji's suddenly entering a monastery, Tenji's son, Ôtomo no Ôji, was raised to the throne as Emperor Kôbun. Ôama raised the flag of revolt, and easily won the day; Kôbun was on the throne for only eight months, and civil war raged the entire time. The hapless Emperor committed suicide in 672. Ôama ascended the throne as Emperor Tenmu. (In fact it was not until 1870 that Kôbun was officially entered onto the roster of those who had sat on the Imperial throne, and was given the posthumous name Kôbun.)

D1: Ôama, the future Emperor Tenmu

In pre-Nara/Heian Japan it was not unknown for the Emperors and members of the Imperial family to wear armour. This *keikô* is one of the more elaborately designed ones to have survived, and though it has never been attributed to Tenmu it is contemporary with him. The gilt helmet is covered with ornate designs. The *keikô* is styled rather like a poncho (a style called *uchikake*) and is sideless; hence the separate sections of scale worn at the sides and donned before the main section. He is shown without the full shoulder guards. (Source: a *keikô* and *en suite* helmet from Kiyokawa-mura Gion Kôfun, Chiba Pref.)

D2: Ôtomo no Makuta

Makuta was a scion of the great Ôtomo clan. At his death in 683 he was awarded a high court rank by Tenmu in recognition of his efforts on the Emperor's behalf. The *tankô* was on its way out, but note this attempt to keep it current by attaching a skirt of scales as for a *keikô*. (Source: *tankô* from Mugyû-mura Kôfun, Fukuoka Pref.)

D3: Ôtomo no Fukei

Fukei, younger brother of Makuta, also supported Ôama in his struggle against Kôbun, commanding in several successful engagements including a decisive battle at Ômi. He was one of those who helped bring about a revival of his clan, whose prestige had suffered through the past defeats in Mimana, long entrusted to the Ôtomo. He died in 683. The final form of the *keikô*, shown here, was the poncho with separate side sections. It was this which would evolve into the later *ô-yoroi*, with the simple wrap-around *keikô* being continued as the *dô-maru*. The helmet is a variation inspired by Chinese/Mongol patterns. It is actually fairly advanced, and is a direct predecessor of later models, combined with the *shukakufu kabuto*, as can be seen in later plates. (Source: an armour excavated from the Hajikami-mura Hajikama-hama Kôfun, Wakayama Pref., and reconstructed by Suenaga)

Plate E: Naramaro's Revolt, 757

Tachibana Naramaro, great-grandson of Shotoku Taishi, grew jealous of Fujiwara Nakamaro and his family's increasing influence. With the aid of several influential friends, he plotted the downfall of Nakamaro, but the minister heard of the plans and had the conspirators taken. They were put to death.

E1: Tachibana Naramaro

Caught unawares, Naramaro here wears his normal garb, the typical daytime clothing of the highest classes of Nara society. The outer robe is a style called *ketteki no hô*, and it is worn over an underrobe, the *hanpi*, and special trousers called *shirokihakama*. The fashions were heavily influenced by continental styles, and virtually identical to garb worn in China. (Source: scroll paintings and a model in the Japan Costume Museum)

E2: Warrior from Nakamaro's house

The *men'ôchû* is a mystery; here we assume that it was a form of plateless padded garment. Most depictions colour it red and yellow, so we have followed convention. Whatever its construction, the *men'ôchû* cannot have been a very comfortable armour to wear. (Source: figurine from China, and Suenaga's studies; author's reconstruction)

E3: Nakamaro's lieutenant

The development from the *keikô* to the *dô-maru* was slow, but this was the likely intermediate step. A few scales, fortunately all laced together and forming a vertical section from the top of the coat to the bottom, are preserved in the Shôsoin; and from these and period illustrations armour historians have made this reconstruction. Despite the transitional state, these armours are still classified as *keikô* (albeit as variations) by modern historians. His horse furniture is in typical Nara style; note that the stirrups have become enclosed. (Source: reconstruction by Sasama Yoshihiko)

Plate F: Tenkei no Ran, 940

Masakado's rebellion against the Heiankyô establishment was finally crushed by a combined force led by his cousin Sadamori. He is supposed to have met his end in an engagement with Fukiwara no Hidesato while attempting to flee; an arrow struck Masakado, and he fell from his horse. Hidesato leapt in and finished him off, sending his head back to the capital for viewing.

F1: Taira no Masakado

His armour here is a late transitional *keikô*, which could probably be called proto-*ô-yoroi*. None has survived, but this reconstruction is a likely development based on the forms which came before and after, and has gained the general support of the Japanese armour historian community. Small changes have occurred in horse furniture; from this point on, changes were mostly cosmetic. (Source: scrolls, and a reconstruction by Sasama)

F2: Taira clan bushi

This warrior wears the other product of the *keikô*, the *dô-maru*. Although it, too, is transitional, much more is known about it, and it is closer to the true *dô-maru* than Masakado's armour is to the *ô-yoroi*. (Source: scrolls, and a reconstruction by Sasama)

This is a common warrior in a dô-maru as might be found in the mid-Kamakura Period. Note the way the gyôyô are used in place of the sode. (Japan Costume Museum)

G: Heian fashions, 1083

Many of the fashions worn at the court in Heiankyô, particularly those for court occasions, are still seen today in Japan with very little alteration of cut or style. They can be seen as the official uniforms of Shinto priests, and of the Imperial Family and high officials when performing official duties and functions. (An excellent example was the enthronement ceremony of the Emperor in 1990, and the wedding of his second son, Prince Akishino, a few months before.)

G1: Courtier in formal dress

This is typical of the ceremonial full dress of the Japanese court even today. His garb is called a *sokutai*, and is the most formal outfit of all. (The black brocade for his *hôeki no hô* is the ultimate in formality—'white tie and tails'.) The *hôeki no hô* is frequently of a translucent black brocade; when of another colour, it is usually opaque. The train, hanging from an under-robe called a *shita-gasane*, is but one indicator of rank. The ornate object hanging from the belt is called a *hiraô*. Not clearly visible due to the overlap of fabric is the black leather belt worn with such garb. In the back, the long end loops up from the right and is tucked down in again on the left. He holds a polished wooden 'sceptre' called a *shaku*. All members of the court aristocracy carried them, though they served no function. The headgear is called *kanmuri*, and is the Japanese equivalent of a coronet or crown. Were this noble to wear an outfit with an identically cut *hôeki no hô* (complete with *shita-gasane*) but trousers as shown in F3, the name of the outfit would become *hôko*, and it would be a grade less formal: say, 'black tie'. With a coloured robe and without the *shita-gasane* (and with F3 trousers) it would be an informal *ikan*, perhaps the equivalent of just a good three-piece suit today. (Source: scroll paintings and a model in the Japan Costume Museum)

G2: Palace guard, duty uniform

The palace guards were often far more than peacocks. Some great warriors were given commissions in the guard, and took their turns walking the corridors and perimeter with pride. It is true that many noble sons were appointed merely for the sake of the title, but they were generally respected. Their position in Heian society—until the Taira took over, at least, but again after the Taira fell—was one of respect. There were a few other crests used, which seem to have been related to duties or assignments, which would make this a sort of uniform—one of the world's first. (Source: scroll paintings and a model in the Japan Costume Museum)

G3: Noble in daytime costume

When relaxing at home or out visiting this is the style of dress commonly worn. The name of the predominant garment—the *kariginu*—has given this outfit its name. It is sideless and poncho-like; the back is worn long while the front is pulled up and allowed to hang over the belt. The trousers are of *sashinuki* style, long and full and gathered at the ankles. (Source: scroll paintings and a model in the Japan Costume Museum)

G4: Court lady in formal attire

This costume can still be seen today at coronations and at other highly formal ceremonies. It is called *jûni-hitoe*, for the 12 layers (*jûni* in Japanese) that supposedly made it up; generally it is more often between six and ten. Each layer of *kimono* was different in colour and pattern, and great care and consideration went into choosing the ones to wear. Ladies' reputations at court could be made or ruined in one day by a particularly skilled or thoughtless selection. Such an outfit could weigh upwards of 15 kilos or more; and considering the deadly humidity of Kyôto summers, it was not a garment made for comfort. (Source: scroll paintings, a model in the Japan Costume Museum, and the wedding garb of Kawashima Kiko, Princess Akishino)

H: Go-Sannen no Eki, 1086

The conflict between the Kiyowara and the Minamoto ended in favour of the Minamoto, but it set a dangerous precedent when the government failed to officially sanction Yoshiie in his struggle on its behalf.

H1: Minamoto no Yoshiie

Yoshiie earned for himself the name Hachiman Tarô while in his teens; he was a fierce warrior and a gifted strategist. Considered as one of the greatest heroes of mediaeval Japan, he is shown here wearing an armour laced in red silk threads. The elaborate helmet crest is a sign of his rank, though the design has no special meaning. Before him is a tray with two kinds of seaweed and chestnuts, ritually significant foods, and he is being brought a special *sake*. This is part of the

A warrior wearing a dô-maru and sode. The gyôyô have been brought forward to protect the frogs holding the shoulder straps to the front of the cuirass. (Japan Costume Museum)

ceremony preparatory to setting off to battle in an age when there was time for such niceties. (Source: a reconstructed *aka-ito odoshi ô-yoroi* in the home of the Hori family)

H2: Warrior monk
In future struggles, notably several engagements of the Genpei War, the *sôhei* would play a major role. The monks' favourite weapon seems to have been the *naginata*, although not a few were also skilled with the sword. He wears basic armour only under his robes—a *dô* of unclear form and lacing—although some monks would also wear armoured sleeves. (Source: battle scrolls)

H3: Minamoto samurai
The samurai bringing ritual *sake* to Yoshiie wears a typical *dô-maru* laced with treated leather thongs. This type of *odoshi* was fairly common in the early period, as it was one of the cheapest available; there are at least two such *dô-maru* classified as valuable objects by the Japanese government. (Source: an Important Cultural Property armour preserved in Oyamazumi Jinja, Aichi Pref.)

I: Dan-no-Ura, 1185
The final great confrontation between the Genji and the Heike was amidst the swirling waters separating Kyûshû and Honshû. The Heike, to lure the Genji out, put their great commanders in smaller boats, leaving the larger, more ostentatious craft to their rank and file. They knew that the Genji commanders would target those boats, so the Heike commanders could surround and surprise them. It is an argument before this battle between Yoshitsune and Kagetoki which is supposed to have led to the Genji leader's later destruction through the latter's jealousy.

I1: Taira no Tomomori
The Taira commander, like many members of his clan, threw himself into the waves when all was lost. Some sources have him tying an anchor about his armour and leaping into the sea, while others

The ô-yoroi could be inconvenient at times. When not needed, the bushi would generally wear only the nodo-wa, kote, suneate, and waidate, collectively called the ko-gu (literally 'small gear'). He could then don his armour quickly. (Japan Costume Museum)

maintain that he donned a second suit of armour. Here he wears an *ô-yoroi* of *ô-arame* (broad scales) laced with leather thong bearing a pattern of cherry blossoms called *ko-zakura odoshi*. (Source: a National Treasure armour preserved at Itsukushima Jinja, Hiroshima Pref.)

I2: Taira no Munemori

The third son of Kiyomori was the classic bully, evil and cowardly. He was one of the male line of the Heike family who survived the battle, but only because he was too frightened to kill himself; he was taken prisoner and executed shortly after. His armour is a type called *dô-maru yoroi*, a sort of mixture between the *dô-maru* and *ô-yoroi* styles in vogue for about 50 years. (Source: a National Treasure armour preserved in Ôyamazumi Jinja, Aichi Pref.)

I3: Taira no Noritsune

Missing an opportunity to kill Yoshitsune in hand-to-hand combat during the battle, Noritsune discarded his helmet and challenged anyone to try to take him. Two brothers, Sanemitsu and Jirô, Genji retainers, charged him; he caught one under each arm and jumped into the sea, taking them with him as he drowned. His armour is laced in *kon-ito-odoshi*, or dark blue silk braided cord. (Source: a National Treasure armour preserved in Itsukushima Jinj, Hiroshima Pref.)

J: Shokyû no Ran, 1221

Emperor Go-Toba's unfortunate attempt to wrest control from the Hôjô *shikken* ended in failure and exile. Among the commanders sent out under the *bakufu* flag was 38-year-old Hôjô Yasutoki, a future *shikken*.

J1: Hôjô samurai

This already-armoured soldier holds Yasutoki's helmet. This was an honour, and helmet bearers (and sandal bearers) were part of the personal staff of most generals on campaign. His simple armour is a *fusubegawa-odoshi* (treated leather) *dô-maru*, typical of the period; it is not overly ornate, nor is it too plain. (Source: an armour preserved at the Izumo Taisha)

J2: Hôjô Yasutoki

Yasutoki was the son of Yoshitoki, second Hôjô *shikken*. In three years Yasutoki's father would die, and he would become *shikken*. His armour is a simple affair, laced in *murasaki susogu ito odoshi* (graded purple silk braid cords). Although almost all surviving instances of such graded armours were purple (*murasaki*), there were also others where the key colour was a dark shade of crimson, blue, or green, which was graded from light at the top to dark at the bottom. An inverted pattern called *nioi-odoshi* was also popular. (Source: an armour in the Tokyo National Museum)

J3: Hôjô retainer

A retainer who wears a *hitatare*, the standard day wear for members of the military class, helps Yasutoki into his armour. There were many varieties of *hitatare*; one with an almost identical cut but much less full sleeves was termed the *yoroi-hitatare* and was worn under armour from the early/mid Heian days right into the Edo Era (1600–1858). *Hitatare* are generally differentiated not so much by cut, which

This youth wears a haramaki-dô over a kariginu. Many wore armour in this way during the Heian and Kamakura Periods. (Japan Costume Museum)

varied little, but by decoration and fabric. (This is almost a rule with many old Japanese items of dress.) Thus, an identical suit of solid colour with perhaps small crests would be termed a *suo*, with large plate-sized crests a *dai-mon* (literally 'great crest'), and so on. A modern relative of the *dai-mon* is worn by referees at *sumô* wrestling. (Source: scroll paintings, the Japan Costume Museum)

K1: Shôni no Kagesuke

The nominal governor of Dazaifu was a skilled commander, organising defences, leading attacks, and rallying his men. He was also merciless; after the typhoon he ruthlessly hunted down shipwrecked Mongols and put them to the sword. His *ô-yoroi* is laced in *asagi-aya-odoshi* (light green silk braided cord). The cape-like object at his back is called a *horo*, and was worn to give an imposing image when

galloping on horseback. Armour outfitters of the late 16th century, seeing pictures of the *horo* on scrolls long after it had fallen out of popularity, revived it; but not knowing its true construction, they used wickerwork baskets to support what looked like fabric balloons. It is believed that the *horo* were, like the tigerskin-covered scabbard here, prerogatives of rank. (Source: National Treasure armour preserved at Itsukushima Jinja, Hiroshima Pref.)

K2: Ashigaru

This low-ranking samurai carries an unusual but very effective weapon called a *nagamaki*, and wears a *hara-ate*. It is not certain when they actually appeared, but probably around this time. The briefest of all Japanese armours, it protected only the belly and groin. There would be many forms, including those with abbreviated *kusazuri*, but contemporary illustrations indicate that the earliest *hara-ate* were probably identical to the front half of a *dô*. Centuries later it would come to be an item for dress wear under the robes by pacified *daimyô* who did not want the inconvenience of full armour. (Source: battle scrolls)

K3: Kyûshû samurai

Far from the capital in Kyôto and the centre of government in Kamakura though it was, Kyûshû had state-of-the-art armour; after the attack in 1274 they needed it. This samurai is depicted in the common armour of the day; his *dô* is laced in *murasaki-gawa odoshi* (purple dyed leather thong). Samurai usually carried heavy daggers specifically designed for taking heads. They were carried handle down and edge forward for ease of drawing, and were double edged; their method of use was to thrust directly through the neck into the ground below and rock the blade left and right. Three were usually carried as they were discardable. It was a particularly nasty weapon in close fighting. (Source: Important Cultural Property armour in Ôyamazumi Jinja, Ehime Pref.)

L: Nanboku-chô, c. 1333

When Ashikaga Takauji took up the cause of the Emperor and joined forces with Kusunoki Masashige and Nitta Yoshisada, it was clear that the *bakufu* was doomed. What had not been expected was that Ashikaga would raise his own banner, and then go to war against his erstwhile comrades, ending their lives

and elevating himself to the highest position in the land. Here they are depicted in happier days, when they were allies.

L1: Ashikaga Takauji

Takauji had an excellent lineage: he was a descendant of Minamoto Yoshiie and his mother was from the Hôjô clan. His armour is based on one which belonged to him, recently discovered in the 'dungeons' of the Metropolitan Museum in New York City. He wears a new addition to the armour of the period: *haidate*. Designed like a split apron, they were useful on horseback, and developed primarily because of the increased use of multi-tasseted *dô*, which offered less in the way of thigh protection to the mounted warrior than did the *ô-yoroi*. Here, the style comes from a famous portrait of Takauji.

L2: Nitta Yoshisada

Nitta is here depicted in a *dô-maru* of *hanada-ito-odoshi* (pale blue silk braided cord). The *shikoro* is one of the most extreme examples of the tendency to make them horizontal, a style called *kasa-jikoro*, or 'umbrella *shikoro*'. The crest holder bears the inscription 'Hachiman Dai Bosatsu' in homage to Hachiman, the Shinto war god (the deified Emperor Ôjin). (Source: Important Cultural Property armour in a private collection)

L3: Kusunoki Masashige

Masashige's armour is of alternating metal and leather scales laced in *kuro-gawa-odoshi* (black leather thong). The scales for the trunk of the *dô* are different from those used for the rest of the armour, consisting of scales with scalloped heads (rather than the typical sloping angled variety) and lie much flatter, exposing more surface with less overlap. Such scales are called *iyo-zane*, and in future years would gain popularity for their relative ease of construction and low cost. They would need to be stronger than the other *kozane*, however, which overlapped for a full half of their surface, resulting in an all-over double layer of scales. (Source: National Treasure armour preserved in Kasuga Taisha, Nara Pref.)

L4: Samurai retainer

The armour worn by this retainer is a *shiro-kinu-tsutsumi haramaki*, a 'white silk wrapped haramaki'. While many armours from this period with the plates so 'wrapped' in leather have survived, very few have come down to us with silk or other cloth in place of leather. During the Edo Period there were a few armours of note made similarly using brocade and damask, but during the Nanboku-chô the material was invariably unpatterned fabric. Note also the use of patterned silk fabric on the *muna-ita* and the *waki-ita*. Like many *haramaki* of the period, there are no attachments for *sode*, implying that this is all there was. While such would tend to indicate a retainer's armour, simple *haramaki* were occasionally worn under other armour—generally an *ô-yoroi*—as an increased measure of protection (though at a huge penalty in discomfort). (Source: a National Treasure armour preserved in Hyôzu Jinja, Shiga Pref.)

D1 Un *keiko* très élaboré que l'on attribue à Tenmu. Le casque doré est couvert de dessins ornés. Il ne porte pas les épaulières complètes. **D2** Il porte un *tankô* qui ne se voyait plus que rarement. Une tentative a été faite pour le garder au goût du jour en attachant une jupe de mailles comme pour un *keiko*. **D3** La forme définitive du *keiko* avec section latérale séparée. Le casque s'inspire de modèles chinois/mongols.

E1 Vêtements de jour caractéristiques des classes supérieures de la société Nara. L'influence de la Chine était vive sur les modes. **E2** Il porte une forme de vêtement rembourré sans plates, le *men'ôchù*. **E3** Il porte un style d'armure intermédiaire entre le *keiko* et le *dô-maru*. L'harnachement du cheval est typique du style Nara.

F1 Ce personnage porte un *keiko* de fin de période de transition qui est presque un proto *ô-yoroi*. **F2** Ce guerrier porte l'autre produit du *keiko*, le *dô-maru*. Il est aussi transitoire mais on en sait plus à son sujet.

G1 Tenue de cérémonie de la cour japonaise. Le *sokutai* est le costume le plus cérémonieux de tous. L'objet très orné suspendu à la ceinture s'appelle un *hiraô*. Le "sceptre" en bois traité s'appelle le *shaku*. La coiffure porte le nom de *kanmuri* et est l'équivalent d'une couronne. **G2** Les gardes du palais étaient généralement hautement respectés et portaient toute une variété de cimiers ayant trait à leurs fonctions – une forme d'uniforme de début de période. **G3** Un noble en costume de jour, pour se détendre chez soi en visite. Le vêtement prédominant a donné son nom au costume: le *kariginu*. **G4** Tenue de cour hautement officielle, elle se nomme *juni-hitoe* et se compose de six à dix couches de kimono choisies avec le plus grand soin.

H1 Armure lacée en fils de soie rouge; la crête de casque élaborée est une marque de rang. Sur le plateau placé devant lui deux genres d'algues et de châtaignes, mets qui ont une signification rituelle, et on lui apporte un sake spécial. Cela fait partie d'une cérémonie avant le départ au combat. **H2** Il porte une armure de base sous ses robes et est armé d'un *naginata*. **H3** Il porte un *dô-maru* caractéristique, lacé avec des lanières de cuir traité.

I1 Ce personnage porte un *ô-yoroi* d'*ô-arame* (larges mailles) lacé avec des lanières de cuir portant un dessin de fleurs de cerisier et appelées *ko-zakura odoshi*. **I2** Cette armure se nomme *dô-maru yoroi*, un mélange de *dô-maru* et d'*ô-yoroi*, en vogue pendant 50 ans environ. **I3** Cette armure est lacée en *kon-ito-odoshi* ou cordon tressé de soie bleue foncée.

J1 Le porteur de casque de Yasutoki, une position de haut rang. Son armure simple est un *fusubegawa-odoshi* (cuir traité) *dô-maru* caractéristique de cette période. **J2** Il porte une simple armure lacée en *Murasaki susogu ito odoshi* (cordons tressés de soie à dégradés de pourpre). **J3** Cette personne de la suite d'un noble porte le *hitatare*, la tenue courante de jour des membres de la classe militaire.

K1 Le *ô-yoroi* de ce personnage est lacé en *asagi-aya-odoshi* (cordon tressé de soie verte pâle). Il porte sur le dos un *horo* qui ressemble à une cape. **K2** Ce samurai de bas rang porte une arme dénommée *nagamaki* avec *hara-ate*, un ensemble limité d'armure. **K3** Ce samurai porte l'armure courante du jour; son *dô* est lacé en *Murasaki-gawa odoshi* (lanière de cuir teinte en pourpre).

L1 Takauji porte une nouvelle addition sur son armure au goût du jour: l'*haidate*. Celle-ci fut mise au point pour monter à cheval. **L2** Nitta porte le *dô-maru hanada-ito-odoshi* (à cordon tressé de soie bleue pâle). **L3** Cette armure est en écailles de métal et de cuir alternées, lacée en *kuro-gawa-odoshi* (lanière de cuir noir). **L4** Ce suivant porte une armure appelée *shiro-kinutsutsumi haramaki*, un "haramaki dont on s'enveloppe en soie blanche". L'armure s'enveloppant autour de corps en "cuir" est très courante à cette période mais la soie est très inhabituelle.

D1 Diese hoch ausgearbeitete *Keiko*-Rüstung wird Tenmu zugeschrieben. Der vergoldete Helm ist mit reichen Verzierungen geschmückt. Die kompletten Schulterstücke werden nicht getragen. **D2** Er trägt einen *Tanko*, der damals immer weniger verwendet wurde. Um ihn "modern" zu machen, wurde wie für den *Keiko* ein Panzerrock hinzugefügt. **D3** Die endgültige Version des *Keiko* mit separaten Seitenteilen. Der Helm ist von chinesisch/mongolischen Vorbildern inspiriert.

E1 Typische Tageskleidung der obersten Klassen der Nara-Gesellschaft. Die Mode wurde stark von China beeinflußt. **E2** Er trägt eine Art von plattenlosem gepolstertem Kleidungsstück, den *Men'ochu*. **E3** Er trägt eine Rüstung, die im Stil zwischen *Keiko* und *Do-maru* liegt. Das Pferdezubehör ist typisch für den Nara-Stil.

F1 Diese Figur zeigt einen späten *Keiko* aus der Übergangszeit – fast ein Vorgänger des *O-yoroi*. **F2** Dieser Krieger trägt das andere Produkt des *Keiko*, den *Do-maru*. Das ist ebenfalls ein Übergangsstück, doch weiß man viel mehr darüber.

G1 Feierliche Kleidung am japanischen Hof. Der *Sokutai* ist das allerformellste Kleidungsstück. Das verzierte Objekt am Gürtel hieß *Hirao*. Das hölzerne "Szepter" hieß *Shaku*. Die Kopfbedeckung wurde *Kanmuri* genannt und ist das Äquivalent einer Krone oder eines Kronreifens. **G2** Die Palastwachen waren allgemein sehr angesehen und trugen verschiedene Abzeichen je nach ihren Aufgaben – eine frühe Art der Uniform. **G3** Ein Aristokrat in Tages-kleidung, getragen zuhause oder wie bei Besuchen. Das vorherrschende Kleidungsstück hat der ganzen Kleidung den Namen gegeben – *Kariginu*. **G4** Sehr formelle Hofkleidung namens *Juni-hitoe*, bestehend aus sechs bis zehn Lagen von Kimono, die sehr sorgfältig ausgewählt wurden.

H1 Rüstung mit roten Seidenschnüren; das komplexe Helmabzeichen zeigt den Rang an. Das Tablett vor ihm enthält zwei Arten von Seetang und Kastanien; das waren rituelle Nahrungsmittel, und man bringt ihm auch einen speziellen Sake. Das ist Teil einer Zeremonie ehe man in den Krieg zog. **H2** Er trägt eine grundlegende Rüstung unter den Gewändern und ist mit einem *Naginata* bewaffnet. **H3** Er trägt ein typisches *Do-maru*, verschnürt mit bearbeiteten Lederriemen.

I1 Diese Figur trägt einen *O-yoroi* aus *O-arame* (breiten Schuppen), verschnürt mit Lederriemen die man im Muster von Kirschblüten, genannt *Ko-zakura odoshi*. **I2** Diese Rüstung ist vom Typ *Do-maru yoroi*, eine Kombination von *Do-maru* und *O-yoroi*; sie wurde etwa 50 Jahre lang getragen. **I3** Diese Rüstung ist mit *kon-ito-odoshi* verschnürt, also mit dunkelblauen, geflochtenen Seidenschnüren.

J1 Yasutokis Helmträger, eine ehrenhafte Position. Sein schlichter Panzer ist ein *Fusubegawa-odoshi* (Leder) *Do-maru*, typisch für die Periode. **J2** Er trägt eine schlichte Rüstung, verschnürt mit *Murasaki susogu ito odoshi* (violette, geflochtene Seidenschnüre). **J3** Dieser Söldner trägt ein *Hitatare*, die normale Tageskleidung von Angehörigen der Militärklasse.

K1 Diese Figur trägt einen *O-yoroi*, verschnürt mit *Asagi-aya-odoshi* (hell-grüne, geflochtene Seidenschnüre). Das umhangartige Kleidungsstück auf dem Rücken heißt *Horo*. **K2** Dieser Samurai niedrigen Ranges trägt eine Waffe namens *Nagamaki* und einen *Hara-ate*, eine Rüstung beschränkter Art. **K3** Dieser Samurai trägt den damals weit verbreiteten Panzer; sein Do ist mit *Murasaki-gawa odoshi* verschnürt, also mit violett gefärbten Lederriemen.

L1 Takauji trägt ein neues Zubehör zur damaligen Rüstung – *Haidate*, entwickelt für die Verwendung zu Pferde. **L2** Nitta trägt Do-maru *Hanada-ito-odoshi* (hellblaue, geflochtene Seidenschnüre). **L3** Diese Rüstung besteht aus abwechselnd angeordneten Metall- und Lederschuppen, verschnürt mit *Kuro-gawa-odoshi* (schwarzen Lederriemen). **L4** Dieser Söldner trägt eine Rüstung namens *Shiro-kinutsutsumi haramaki*, einen mit weißer Seide umhüllten Haramaki. Lederumhüllte Rüstungen waren in dieser Periode weit verbreitet, Seide hingegen war höchst ungewöhnlich.